OXFORD STUI

Series Editor: S

Robert Browning

Selected Poems

Edited by Julia Geddes

Oxford University Press

OXFORD
UNIVERSITY PRESS

Great Clarendon Street, Oxford OX2 6DP

Oxford University Press is a department of the University of Oxford.
It furthers the University's objective of excellence in research, scholarship,
and education by publishing worldwide in

Oxford   New York

Auckland   Cape Town   Dar es Salaam   Hong Kong   Karachi
Kuala Lumpur   Madrid   Melbourne   Mexico City   Nairobi
New Delhi   Shanghai   Taipei   Toronto

With offices in

Argentina   Austria   Brazil   Chile   Czech Republic   France   Greece
Guatemala   Hungary   Italy   Japan   South Korea   Poland   Portugal
Singapore   Switzerland   Thailand   Turkey   Ukraine   Vietnam

Oxford is a registered trade mark of Oxford University Press
in the UK and in certain other countries

British Library Cataloguing in Publication Data

Data available

ISBN: 978-0-19-8310761

1 3 5 7 9 10 8 6 4 2

Typeset in India by TNQ Books and Journals Pvt. Ltd.

Printed in China by Printplus

Paper used in the production of this book is a natural, recyclable product made from wood
grown in sustainable forests. The manufacturing process conforms to the environmental
regulations of the country of origin.

The publishers would like to thank the following for permission to reproduce photographs:

Pages 3, 7 and 200: Mary Evans Picture Library; page 8: Italian School (15th century)/
Florence, Tuscany, Italy/Guido Mannucci/The Bridgeman Art Library; page 153: The
National Gallery, London; page 161: Birmingham Museums and Art Gallery; page 176:
National Gallery of Scotland, Edinburgh, Scotland/The Bridgeman Art Library; page 186:
Sacred Destinations; page 195: SuperStock/Getty Images; page 201: Dean and Chapter of
Westminster.

Contents

Acknowledgements

The text of the poems and the extract from the letter to Elizabeth Barrett are from *Robert Browning: The Major Works*, edited by Adam Roberts and Daniel Karlin (Oxford World's Classics, 2009); other poems: *Home-Thoughts, from Abroad* and *The Patriot* are from *Browning's Shorter Poems*, edited by Franklin T. Baker (Macmillan, 1917) and *The Last Ride Together* and *A Woman's Last Word* are from *The Poems of Robert Browning 1847–1861*, edited by John Woolford, Daniel Karlin and Joseph Phelan (Pearson Education, 2007).

Extracts from the *Authorized Version of the Bible* (*The King James Bible*), the rights in which are vested in the Crown, are reproduced by permission of the Crown's Patentee, Cambridge University Press.

Acknowledgements from Julia Geddes
I would like to thank my husband David Barton for his support and proof reading of the work as it took shape over the past year. I am also indebted to my daughter Madeleine for access to Balliol College Library where some of the original manuscripts can be found. Finally, I would like to thank Jan Doorly for her patience, help and insight throughout the writing of this text, and Steven Croft for his encouragement and advice.

Editors

Steven Croft, the series editor, holds degrees from Leeds and Sheffield universities. He has taught at secondary and tertiary level and headed the Department of English and Humanities in a tertiary college. He has 25 years' examining experience at A level and is currently a Principal Examiner for English. He has written several books on teaching English at A level, and his publications for Oxford University Press include *Exploring Literature*, *Success in AQA Language and Literature* and *Exploring Language and Literature*.

Julia Geddes has a degree in English and Philosophy, and an MA in English Literature from the University of Leeds. She is currently Head of English in a large sixth form college in the north of England. She is also a Senior Examiner and Moderator and has been the author of several study guides for A level students. She presents conferences for students and provides support for teachers working with A level specifications.

Foreword

Oxford Student Texts, under the founding editorship of Victor Lee, have established a reputation for presenting literary texts to students in both a scholarly and an accessible way. The new editions aim to build on this successful approach. They have been written to help students, particularly those studying English literature for AS or A level, to develop an increased understanding of their texts. Each volume in the series, which covers a selection of key poetry and drama texts, consists of four main sections which link together to provide an integrated approach to the study of the text.

The first part provides important background information about the writer, his or her times and the factors that played an important part in shaping the work. This discussion sets the work in context and explores some key contextual factors.

This section is followed by the poetry or play itself. The text is presented without accompanying notes so that students can engage with it on their own terms without the influence of secondary ideas. To encourage this approach, the Notes are placed in the third section, immediately following the text. The Notes provide explanations of particular words, phrases, images, allusions and so forth, to help students gain a full understanding of the text. They also raise questions or highlight particular issues or ideas which are important to consider when arriving at interpretations.

The fourth section, Interpretations, goes on to discuss a range of issues in more detail. This involves an examination of the influence of contextual factors as well as looking at such aspects as language and style, and various critical views or interpretations. A range of activities for students to carry out, together with discussions as to how these might be approached, are integrated into this section.

At the end of each volume there is a selection of Essay Questions, a Further Reading list and, where appropriate, a Glossary.

We hope you enjoy reading this text and working with these supporting materials, and wish you every success in your studies.

Steven Croft   *Series Editor*

Robert Browning in Context

The early years

Robert Browning was born in Camberwell, London in 1812 and was on the whole self-taught; he received little formal education after the age of 14. He is best known for his poems in the form of dramatic monologues, many of which are included in this collection. After his marriage to the poet Elizabeth Barrett, he moved to Florence in Italy, and this period proved to be the most richly productive of his life. The move to Italy stimulated his interest in Renaissance art and artists, and we can see this reflected in the poems *Pictor Ignotus*, *Fra Lippo Lippi* and *Andrea del Sarto* in this selection.

At the time of Browning's birth, Britain had been at war with France for 20 years and the climax to this conflict was fast approaching. By 1814 Napoleon, the French emperor, had abdicated and been exiled, but he escaped and was finally defeated at the battle of Waterloo on 18 June 1815. It was into a Britain that was exhausted and impoverished by wars but immensely empowered by the acquisition of a new empire that Browning was born. This era also saw the births of the naturalist Charles Darwin, who was to revolutionize scientific and religious thought with his theory of evolution, and the great writers Charles Dickens, William Makepeace Thackeray, and Alfred, Lord Tennyson. The second generation of Romantic poets was becoming established: Lord Byron published the first two cantos of *Childe Harold* in 1812; in the previous year Percy Bysshe Shelley (a poet who was to greatly influence Browning in his early writing) had been sent down from Oxford for his atheism; and in 1816 John Keats gave up his budding medical career to concentrate on his poetry.

By the time Browning was 14 he had completed his schooling but, unlike many of his contemporary writers and artists, he was not compelled to work for a living. He was encouraged by an indulgent father to make use of his extensive library at home in order to develop his love of literature and his aptitude for verse-making. Browning was fond of walking and his father was keen to ensure he had all the skills required of a gentleman, so he was given instruction in riding and fencing. These physical activities were to provide him with a rich source of imagery in his poetry.

As a religious Nonconformist (outside the Church of England), Browning was barred from attending Oxford or Cambridge universities. However, London University had recently opened and, since it had no conditions about religious observance, Browning began attending in 1828. But having set out on a course of study in Classics and German, he found he disliked the teaching and also missed his home, so within six months he had given up his place and returned to the family home.

Browning was very attached to his father and he clearly respected his attitudes and values, but it was his mother who provided him with emotional support. He was devoted to her and was grief-stricken at her death in 1849, a week after the birth of his son Pen. She was a deeply religious woman and his rebellion against Christian teaching in the early years of his life must have been difficult both for himself and his mother. As a young boy Browning was deeply religious, but as he became more immersed in Shelley's poetry he rebelled against formal religion. Perhaps his return to religious commitment in later life was influenced by his mother's example.

Browning's first works

Browning's first published work was *Pauline*, a romantic, confessional poem influenced by his love of Byron and other Romantic poets, and works he found in his father's library such as Homer and the ancient Greek dramatists. The publication of *Pauline* in 1833 was financed by Browning's aunt. Its hero is a poet, and its subject is the spiritual biography of the speaker during his early

Robert Browning in Rome in 1859, in a drawing by
Rudolf Lehmann

life, and his salvation, which is attributed to the silent heroine
Pauline. The speaker tells the heroine of the loss of idealism and
sense of purpose, but gradually under her influence he is able to
rise above his pride and self-absorption and turn once more to
God and poetry. The speaker presents Pauline as his spiritual
salvation and one who will act as a guide. The poem concludes
with an invocation to Shelley, whom he calls 'Sun-treader' and
who acts as a symbol for the speaker of his striving towards God
by means of truth and love. The speaker defiantly asserts:

> Sun-treader, I believe in God, and truth
> And love...
> Know my last state is happy – free from doubt,
> Or touch of fear. Love me and wish me well!

Pauline received varied reviews, but Browning was particularly
affected by the reaction of the philosopher John Stuart Mill,
who wrote that the poet had 'considerable poetic powers' but

was 'possessed with a more intense and morbid self-conscious-ness than I ever knew in any sane human being'. Browning vowed never to reveal himself and his spiritual development in his poetry again, insisting that any future work would be dramatic, the speech of imaginary characters and not the musings of Robert Browning.

However, Browning continued to be influenced by Shelley throughout his life. Like earlier Romantic poets, Shelley had been committed to the idea that the poet's creative powers and the way he exercises them reflect God's act of creation. This idea became increasingly unfashionable in the Victorian era, but throughout his life Browning maintained an insistence on the importance of meaning and the value of the powers of the imagi-nation, as distinct from intellectual powers.

It was the poem *Paracelsus* – which seems more like a drama because there are several speakers – that first brought Browning fame. In 1834 Browning had been thinking of a career in diplo-macy, but instead he channelled his efforts into the composition of a poem about the life of Paracelsus, a sixteenth-century Swiss physician and alchemist. The poem is divided into five sections and contains no action, but centres around a dialogue between Paracelsus and his friends. Each section relates to a period in the philosopher's life, but the real subject matter is the protagonist's mental development.

Paracelsus was published at Browning's father's expense. The poem received mixed reviews, the most enthusiastic being that of John Forster in *The Examiner*; others were less complimentary. Although it was a financial failure, the publication of *Paracelsus* brought him into the world of letters and made him some influ-ential friends. He met well-known figures including the poet William Wordsworth and the actor William Macready; the meet-ing with Macready influenced Browning to write for the stage. However, the fact that Browning was far more concerned with motive than with action did not make for popular drama; his play *Strafford* was performed in 1837 with Macready in the title role, but was not successful.

Browning visited Italy for the first time in 1838. Italy at this time was not a united country but a collection of small independent states under various rulers. Browning travelled from Trieste to Venice, admiring the countryside as well as the Alps. On his return he felt he was ready to complete *Sordello*, and it was finally published in 1840 after several years of intermittent work. However, Browning's endless revisions had made it increasingly obscure. The final version, 6000 lines of heroic verse, was not well received; critics described it as characterized by affectation and digression, and even as hysterical. What was worse was that the poem became something of a joke in literary circles. Tennyson asserted that he could only understand two lines, the first and the last. In a letter to Thomas Carlyle, the Scottish satirical author, who had written to him encouragingly, Browning clearly accepted his failure, saying: 'You say roses and lilies and lilac-bunches and lemon-flowers about it while everybody else pelts cabbage stump after potato-paring.' Poor reviews and ridicule damaged Browning's reputation as a rising poet.

Thus for Browning the Victorian age (which dawned in 1837 when on the death of King William IV his 18-year-old niece Victoria succeeded to the throne) had a bad beginning. Victoria's reign was to see dramatic changes and events such as famine and rebellion in Ireland, revolution on the Continent, and the coming of the railways and the penny post. There was also unrest that led to the Chartist movement, which demanded parliamentary reform, and campaigns for the repeal of the Corn Laws, which kept food prices high by imposing duties on imported grain. In the literary world Wordsworth, who had lost his early revolutionary views, became Poet Laureate in 1843. He was now the only surviving writer from the Romantic period.

Browning's reputation may have suffered because of *Sordello* but he nevertheless maintained friendships with many influential people. One of the most important was John Kenyon, an old school friend of Browning's father. He was a wealthy man who encouraged promising writers including Elizabeth Barrett. In 1838 she had published *The Seraphim and Other Poems*, for which she had been acclaimed as 'a genuine poetess of no common order'. In 1842 she published *The Cry of the Children*, in which she depicted the hardships of the working people, including children, under the unregulated capitalist system that had developed with the industrial revolution.

April 1841 saw Browning publish the first of a series entitled *Bells and Pomegranates*, which included some of the work that was to enhance his reputation as a poet, and which saw him moving closer to the dramatic monologue and the shorter narrative poem. The title of the series puzzled many contemporary readers; it is taken from Exodus 28:33–44, where Moses is instructed about the decoration of the garment the priest must wear to approach the altar: 'thou shalt make pomegranates of blue, and of purple, and of scarlet, round about the hem thereof; and bells of gold between them round about: a golden bell and a pomegranate, a golden bell and a pomegranate, upon the hem of the robe round about.' In Volume 8 of the series the reader is offered the following explanation: 'I only meant by that title to indicate an endeavour towards something like an alternation, or mixture, of music with discoursing, sound with sense, poetry with thought; which looks too ambitious when expressed, so the symbol was preferred.'

Some of the poems selected for this book were in Volumes 3 and 7. Volume 3, entitled *Dramatic Lyrics*, consisted of 16 poems, including *My Last Duchess* and *Porphyria's Lover*. The latter had already appeared in the *Monthly Repository* of January 1836. Browning had now found a form that exactly suited his genius: the dramatic monologue.

Elizabeth Barrett

The relationship between Elizabeth Barrett and Robert Browning is one of the most famous in literary history. Elizabeth Barrett was a sensitive and passionate young woman who withdrew into

Elizabeth Barrett Browning in 1859, in a drawing by Field Talfourd

isolation and neurotic illness. This behaviour has been explained by family bereavements and by the fact that her father, a widower, dominated his children and saw any attempt at independence as a sign of monstrous ingratitude. He could not accept the idea of marriage for any of them, and his possessiveness with Elizabeth meant that he kept her closely under his influence. She spent most of her time in her room, seeing few visitors.

It was from this suffocating atmosphere that Robert Browning released his future wife. Initially he wrote to her praising her poetry, but also declaring his love for her personally, although they had never met (see page 158). Their mutual friend Kenyon arranged a meeting in May 1845 and the relationship blossomed. Elizabeth had persuaded herself that she was unable to take an active part in life, but with endless patience Browning helped her to gain confidence and his love gave her back the will to live. She wrote to him, 'I have been drawn back into life by your means and for you... I have come back for you alone... I have come back to live a little for you.' By 1846 Elizabeth was strong enough

7

to defy her father and marry Browning, in St Marylebone Parish Church. He was 34 and she was 40. A week later they left for Italy, where they were to spend most of the 16 years of their married life. Her father refused to forgive her or to see her again, or even to open her letters.

Italy

In 1847 Browning and his wife took up residence in Florence in the Casa Guidi near the Palazzo Pitti. The following year, 1848, was to prove the year of revolutions across Europe. France once again expelled its king, the Czechs and Hungarians rose up against Austrian rule, and in Italy Ferdinand of Naples, the new Pope Pius IX, the Grand Duke Leopold of Tuscany and Charles Albert of Piedmont all granted constitutional reform. However, by 1849 the old forms of reactionary government had been

The Brownings lived in Casa Guidi in Florence

reinstated, and it would be more than a decade before Victor Emmanuel II, who replaced his father Charles Albert, would unify Italy under the crown of Piedmont.

In 1849, at the age of 43, Elizabeth gave birth to their only child, a son called Robert Wiedemann, whom they nicknamed Penini or Pen. By 1852 Browning was writing *'Childe Roland to the Dark Tower Came'*. It is a poem that Browning always claimed had no allegorical significance, yet it does seem to represent the spiritual courage he so much admired. In contrast to the nightmare world of Childe Roland came the dream-like *Love Among the Ruins*, a poem notable for its alternating long and short musical lines. 1853 proved a very productive year for Browning. In Florence he had immersed himself in the Renaissance painting, sculpture and architecture of the city, and read about the painters' lives; he was inspired by his love of art, and also music, to write some of his greatest poems. He told his friend Joseph Milsand: 'I have not left the house one evening since our return. I am writing – a first step towards popularity for me – lyrics with more music and painting than before, so as to get people to hear and see.'

Men and Women

In 1855 Browning published *Men and Women*, the collection from which many of the poems in this selection are taken. It is not easy for us to understand the reactions it provoked among its first readers, as it was damned as being 'energy wasted and power misspent', with one reviewer exclaiming 'This sort of thing should be stopped... madness and mysticism... a nonsensical book'.

Today the poems in *Men and Women* are regarded as showing Browning at the peak of his powers. In most of them it is dramatic characters who speak, rather than Browning's own voice, and the reader is offered a variety of moods and a corresponding diversity of form and poetic metre. *Andrea del Sarto* and *Fra Lippo Lippi* were the direct result of Browning's reading about the lives of famous painters; in *The Last Ride Together*, he explores ideas concerning the contrast between life and art; and *The Patriot* perhaps presents the reader with a satirical comment on the revolutionary years of 1848–1849, with their initial sense of triumph but ultimate failure. The epilogue that concludes *Men and Women*, entitled *One Word More*, dedicates the poems to 'E.B.B.', his wife:

> Love, you saw me gather men and women,
> Live or dead or fashioned by my fancy,
> Enter each and all, and use their service,
> Speak from every mouth, – the speech, a poem...
> Let me speak this once in my true person,
> Not as Lippo, Roland, or Andrea,
> Though the fruit of speech be just this sentence:
> Pray you, look on these my men and women,
> Take and keep my fifty poems finished;
> Where my heart lies, let my brain lie also!

Widowhood

On 17 March 1861, Victor Emmanuel II became the first king of a united Italy. In the previous June, Browning had bought from a small stall in Florence the old yellow book that was to provide the source material for his next major work, *The Ring and the Book*.

The death of Elizabeth on 29 June 1861 left Browning bereft. In a letter to his sister Sarianna he describes her passing and concludes: 'She is with God, who takes from me the life of my life in one sense – not so in the truest. My life is fixed and sure now.' He probably wrote *Prospice* (page 81) shortly afterwards.

The Ring and the Book was completed after the death of Elizabeth and published in 1868. It proved to be the longest and arguably the most complex of all Browning's writings. It is made up of a series of dramatic monologues spoken by a variety of characters who are all concerned in the trial of Count Guido Franceschini for the murder of his wife. It is based on a real case in seventeenth-century Italy. Interestingly, in the opening section (*The Ring and the Book*) and the closing section (*The Book and the Ring*) Browning speaks in his own voice to the reader and explains the title of the poem. In doing so he reveals one of his main beliefs about the creation of his poetry. He offers the reader the metaphor of the Italian ring, which is made from a mixture of pure gold and alloy. When the shape of the ring has been made, acid is sprayed onto the surface, the alloy is dissolved and what remains is the pure gold. Browning says that this process is parallel to the creation of his poetry. He argues that he has taken the equivalent of the gold, which for him is fact or truth, and with it he has mixed his fancy or imagination. Finally he takes away his own personality, thus leaving pure truth in the poem. The process can be described as a reflection, in human terms, of divine creation; Browning asserts that human creativity can: 'Mimic creation, galvanism for life,/ But still a glory portioned in the scale' (*The Ring and the Book* 740–741). Browning saw the task of the poet, like that of all humanity, as the attempt to imitate God as far as human capacities will allow.

In the years following the death of his wife, Browning lived mainly in London. He continued to write and at last gained the recognition he had hoped for. In 1867 the University of Oxford awarded him an honorary degree and he became an honorary fellow of Balliol College. In 1881 a Browning Society was established to promote the study of his work.

However, although he continued to write and publish, none of his later work is regarded as equalling the quality of the poetry written while he lived and wrote with Elizabeth in Italy. Browning died on 12 December 1889 at the age of 77, having written his own epitaph in the epilogue to the collection *Asolando*, published at the time of his death:

> 'Strive and thrive!' cry 'Speed, – fight on, fare ever
> There as here!'

He had hoped to be buried in Florence beside his wife, but the cemetery had been closed to new burials, so on 31 December he was buried in Westminster Abbey (see illustration on page 201). He now lies close to some of the greatest poets in the English language.

Selected Poems of Robert Browning

My Last Duchess

Ferrara

That's my last Duchess painted on the wall,
Looking as if she were alive. I call
That piece a wonder, now: Frà Pandolf's hands
Worked busily a day, and there she stands.
5   Will't please you sit and look at her? I said
'Frà Pandolf' by design, for never read
Strangers like you that pictured countenance,
The depth and passion of its earnest glance,
But to myself they turned (since none puts by
10   The curtain I have drawn for you, but I)
And seemed as they would ask me, if they durst,
How such a glance came there; so, not the first
Are you to turn and ask thus. Sir, 'twas not
Her husband's presence only, called that spot
15   Of joy into the Duchess' cheek: perhaps
Frà Pandolf chanced to say 'Her mantle laps
Over my lady's wrist too much,' or 'Paint
Must never hope to reproduce the faint
Half-flush that dies along her throat:' such stuff
20   Was courtesy, she thought, and cause enough
For calling up that spot of joy. She had
A heart – how shall I say? – too soon made glad,
Too easily impressed; she liked whate'er
She looked on, and her looks went everywhere.
25   Sir, 'twas all one! My favour at her breast,

The dropping of the daylight in the West,
The bough of cherries some officious fool
Broke in the orchard for her, the white mule
She rode with round the terrace – all and each

30   Would draw from her alike the approving speech,
Or blush, at least. She thanked men, – good!
       but thanked
Somehow – I know not how – as if she ranked
My gift of a nine-hundred-years-old name
With anybody's gift. Who'd stoop to blame

35   This sort of trifling? Even had you skill
In speech – (which I have not) – to make
      your will
Quite clear to such an one, and say, 'Just this
Or that in you disgusts me; here you miss,
Or there exceed the mark' – and if she let

40   Herself be lessoned so, nor plainly set
Her wits to yours, forsooth, and made excuse,
– E'en then would be some stooping;
      and I choose
Never to stoop. Oh sir, she smiled, no doubt,
Whene'er I passed her; but who passed without

45   Much the same smile? This grew; I gave commands;
Then all smiles stopped together. There she stands
As if alive. Will't please you rise? We'll meet
The company below, then. I repeat,
The Count your master's known munificence

50   Is ample warrant that no just pretence
Of mine for dowry will be disallowed;
Though his fair daughter's self, as I avowed
At starting, is my object. Nay, we'll go
Together down, sir. Notice Neptune, though,

55   Taming a sea-horse, thought a rarity,
Which Claus of Innsbruck cast in bronze for me!

Porphyria's Lover

The rain set early in to-night,
   The sullen wind was soon awake,
It tore the elm-tops down for spite,
   And did its worst to vex the lake:
5   I listened with heart fit to break.
When glided in Porphyria; straight
   She shut the cold out and the storm,
And kneeled and made the cheerless grate
   Blaze up, and all the cottage warm;
10   Which done, she rose, and from her form
Withdrew the dripping cloak and shawl,
   And laid her soiled gloves by, untied
Her hat and let the damp hair fall,
   And, last, she sat down by my side
15   And called me. When no voice replied,
She put my arm about her waist,
   And made her smooth white shoulder bare,
And all her yellow hair displaced,
   And, stooping, made my cheek lie there,
20   And spread, o'er all, her yellow hair,
Murmuring how she loved me – she
   Too weak, for all her heart's endeavour,
To set its struggling passion free
   From pride, and vainer ties dissever,
25   And give herself to me for ever.
But passion sometimes would prevail,
   Nor could to-night's gay feast restrain
A sudden thought of one so pale
   For love of her, and all in vain:
30   So, she was come through wind and rain.
Be sure I looked up at her eyes

Happy and proud; at last I knew
Porphyria worshipped me; surprise
    Made my heart swell, and still it grew
35   While I debated what to do.
That moment she was mine, mine, fair,
    Perfectly pure and good: I found
A thing to do, and all her hair
    In one long yellow string I wound
40   Three times her little throat around,
And strangled her. No pain felt she;
    I am quite sure she felt no pain.
As a shut bud that holds a bee,
    I warily oped her lids: again
45   Laughed the blue eyes without a stain.
And I untightened next the tress
    About her neck; her cheek once more
Blushed bright beneath my burning kiss:
    I propped her head up as before,
50   Only, this time my shoulder bore
Her head, which droops upon it still:
    The smiling rosy little head,
So glad it has its utmost will,
    That all it scorned at once is fled,
55   And I, its love, am gained instead!
Porphyria's love: she guessed not how
    Her darling one wish would be heard.
And thus we sit together now,
    And all night long we have not stirred,
60   And yet God has not said a word!

Pictor Ignotus

Florence, 15 –

I could have painted pictures like that youth's
   Ye praise so. How my soul springs up! No bar
Stayed me – ah, thought which saddens while it
      soothes!
   – Never did fate forbid me, star by star,
5   To outburst on your night with all my gift
   Of fires from God: nor would my flesh have
      shrunk
From seconding my soul, with eyes uplift
   And wide to heaven, or, straight like thunder,
      sunk
To the centre, of an instant; or around
10   Turned calmly and inquisitive, to scan
The licence and the limit, space and bound,
   Allowed to truth made visible in man.
And, like that youth ye praise so, all I saw,
   Over the canvas could my hand have flung,
15   Each face obedient to its passion's law,
   Each passion clear proclaimed without a tongue;
Whether Hope rose at once in all the blood,
   A-tiptoe for the blessing of embrace,
Or Rapture drooped the eyes, as when her brood
20   Pull down the nesting dove's heart to its place;
Or Confidence lit swift the forehead up,
   And locked the mouth fast, like a castle braved, –
O human faces, hath it spilt, my cup?
   What did ye give me that I have not saved?
25   Nor will I say I have not dreamed (how well!)
   Of going – I, in each new picture, – forth,
As, making new hearts beat and bosoms swell,
   To Pope or Kaiser, East, West, South, or North,

Bound for the calmly-satisfied great State,
30   Or glad aspiring little burgh, it went,
Flowers cast upon the car which bore the freight,
    Through old streets named afresh from the
        event,
Till it reached home, where learned age should greet
    My face, and youth, the star not yet distinct
35   Above his hair, lie learning at my feet! –
    Oh, thus to live, I and my picture, linked
With love about, and praise, till life should end,
    And then not go to heaven, but linger here,
Here on my earth, earth's every man my friend, –
40   The thought grew frightful, 'twas so wildly dear!
But a voice changed it. Glimpses of such sights
    Have scared me, like the revels through a door
Of some strange house of idols at its rites!
    This world seemed not the world it was before:
45   Mixed with my loving trusting ones, there trooped
    ...Who summoned those cold faces that begun
To press on me and judge me? Though I stooped
    Shrinking, as from the soldiery a nun,
They drew me forth, and spite of me... enough!
50   These buy and sell our pictures, take and give,
Count them for garniture and household-stuff,
    And where they live needs must our pictures
        live
And see their faces, listen to their prate,
    Partakers of their daily pettiness,
55   Discussed of, – 'This I love, or this I hate,
    This likes me more, and this affects me less!'
Wherefore I chose my portion. If at whiles
    My heart sinks, as monotonous I paint
These endless cloisters and eternal aisles
60   With the same series, Virgin, Babe and Saint,
With the same cold calm beautiful regard, –

At least no merchant traffics in my heart;
The sanctuary's gloom at least shall ward
    Vain tongues from where my pictures stand
        apart:
65 Only prayer breaks the silence of the shrine
    While, blackening in the daily candle-smoke,
They moulder on the damp wall's travertine,
    'Mid echoes the light footstep never woke.
So, die my pictures! surely, gently die!
70   O youth, men praise so, – holds their praise its
        worth?
Blown harshly, keeps the trump its golden cry?
    Tastes sweet the water with such specks of earth?

The Lost Leader

I

Just for a handful of silver he left us,
    Just for a riband to stick in his coat –
Found the one gift of which fortune bereft us,
    Lost all the others she lets us devote;
5 They, with the gold to give, doled him out silver,
    So much was theirs who so little allowed:
How all our copper had gone for his service!
    Rags – were they purple, his heart had been
        proud!
We that had loved him so, followed him,
        honoured him,
10   Lived in his mild and magnificent eye,
Learned his great language, caught his clear
        accents,

Made him our pattern to live and to die!
Shakespeare was of us, Milton was for us,
   Burns, Shelley, were with us, – they watch from
      their graves!
15 He alone breaks from the van and the freemen,
   – He alone sinks to the rear and the slaves!

II

We shall march prospering, – not thro' his
      presence;
   Songs may inspirit us, – not from his lyre;
Deeds will be done, – while he boasts his
      quiescence,
20   Still bidding crouch whom the rest bade aspire:
Blot out his name, then, record one lost soul more,
   One task more declined, one more footpath
      untrod,
One more devils'-triumph and sorrow for angels,
   One wrong more to man, one more insult to God!
25 Life's night begins: let him never come back to us!
   There would be doubt, hesitation and pain,
Forced praise on our part – the glimmer of
      twilight,
   Never glad confident morning again!
Best fight on well, for we taught him – strike
      gallantly,
30   Menace our heart ere we master his own;
Then let him receive the new knowledge and wait
      us,
   Pardoned in heaven, the first by the throne!

Home-Thoughts, from Abroad

I

Oh, to be in England
Now that April's there,
And whoever wakes in England
Sees, some morning, unaware,
5   That the lowest boughs and the brushwood sheaf
Round the elm-tree bole are in tiny leaf,
While the chaffinch sings on the orchard bough
In England – now!

II

And after April, when May follows,
10   And the white-throat builds, and all the swallows!
Hark I where my blossomed pear tree in the hedge
Leans to the field and scatters on the clover
Blossoms and dewdrops – at the bent spray's
      edge –
That's the wise thrush; he sings each song
      twice over,
15   Lest you should think he never could recapture
The first fine careless rapture!
And though the fields look rough with hoary dew,
All will be gay when noontide wakes anew
The buttercups, the little children's dower
20   – Far brighter than this gaudy melon-flower!

The Bishop Orders His Tomb at Saint Praxed's Church

Rome, 15 –

Vanity, saith the preacher, vanity!
Draw round my bed: is Anselm keeping back?
Nephews – sons mine... ah God, I know not!
    Well –
She, men would have to be your mother once,

5   Old Gandolf envied me, so fair she was!
What's done is done, and she is dead beside,
Dead long ago, and I am Bishop since,
And as she died so must we die ourselves,
And thence ye may perceive the world's a dream.

10   Life, how and what is it? As here I lie
In this state-chamber, dying by degrees,
Hours and long hours in the dead night, I ask
'Do I live, am I dead?' Peace, peace seems all.
Saint Praxed's ever was the church for peace;

15   And so, about this tomb of mine. I fought
With tooth and nail to save my niche, ye know:
– Old Gandolf cozened me, despite my care;
Shrewd was that snatch from out the corner South
He graced his carrion with, God curse the same!

20   Yet still my niche is not so cramped but thence
One sees the pulpit o' the epistle-side,
And somewhat of the choir, those silent seats,
And up into the aery dome where live
The angels, and a sunbeam's sure to lurk:

25   And I shall fill my slab of basalt there,
And 'neath my tabernacle take my rest,
With those nine columns round me, two and two,
The odd one at my feet where Anselm stands:
Peach-blossom marble all, the rare, the ripe

30   As fresh-poured red wine of a mighty pulse.
    – Old Gandolf with his paltry onion-stone,
    Put me where I may look at him! True peach,
    Rosy and flawless: how I earned the prize!
    Draw close: that conflagration of my church
35   – What then? So much was saved if aught were
           missed!
    My sons, ye would not be my death? Go dig
    The white-grape vineyard where the oil-press stood,
    Drop water gently till the surface sink,
    And if ye find... Ah God, I know not, I!...
40   Bedded in store of rotten fig-leaves soft,
    And corded up in a tight olive-frail,
    Some lump, ah God, of *lapis lazuli*,
    Big as a Jew's head cut off at the nape,
    Blue as a vein o'er the Madonna's breast...
45   Sons, all have I bequeathed you, villas, all,
    That brave Frascati villa with its bath,
    So, let the blue lump poise between my knees,
    Like God the Father's globe on both his hands
    Ye worship in the Jesu Church so gay,
50   For Gandolf shall not choose but see and burst!
    Swift as a weaver's shuttle fleet our years:
    Man goeth to the grave, and where is he?
    Did I say basalt for my slab, sons? Black –
    'Twas ever antique-black I meant! How else
55   Shall ye contrast my frieze to come beneath?
    The bas-relief in bronze ye promised me,
    Those Pans and Nymphs ye wot of, and perchance
    Some tripod, thyrsus, with a vase or so,
    The Saviour at his sermon on the mount,
60   Saint Praxed in a glory, and one Pan
    Ready to twitch the Nymph's last garment off,
    And Moses with the tables... but I know

Ye mark me not! What do they whisper thee,
Child of my bowels, Anselm? Ah, ye hope
65 To revel down my villas while I gasp
Bricked o'er with beggar's mouldy travertine
Which Gandolf from his tomb-top chuckles at!
Nay, boys, ye love me – all of jasper, then!
'Tis jasper ye stand pledged to, lest I grieve
70 My bath must needs be left behind, alas!
One block, pure green as a pistachio-nut,
There's plenty jasper somewhere in the world –
And have I not Saint Praxed's ear to pray
Horses for ye, and brown Greek manuscripts,
75 And mistresses with great smooth marbly limbs?
– That's if ye carve my epitaph aright,
Choice Latin, picked phrase, Tully's every word,
No gaudy ware like Gandolf's second line –
Tully, my masters? Ulpian serves his need!
80 And then how I shall lie through centuries,
And hear the blessed mutter of the mass,
And see God made and eaten all day long,
And feel the steady candle-flame, and taste
Good strong thick stupefying incense-smoke!
85 For as I lie here, hours of the dead night,
Dying in state and by such slow degrees,
I fold my arms as if they clasped a crook,
And stretch my feet forth straight as stone
          can point,
And let the bedclothes, for a mortcloth, drop
90 Into great laps and folds of sculptor's-work:
And as yon tapers dwindle, and strange thoughts
Grow, with a certain humming in my ears,
About the life before I lived this life,
And this life too, popes, cardinals and priests,
95 Saint Praxed at his sermon on the mount,
Your tall pale mother with her talking eyes,

And new-found agate urns as fresh as day,
And marble's language, Latin pure, discreet,
– Aha, ELUCESCEBAT quoth our friend?
100 No Tully, said I, Ulpian at the best!
Evil and brief hath been my pilgrimage.
All *lapis*, all, sons! Else I give the Pope
My villas! Will ye ever eat my heart?
Ever your eyes were as a lizard's quick,
105 They glitter like your mother's for my soul,
Or ye would heighten my impoverished frieze,
Piece out its starved design, and fill my vase
With grapes, and add a vizor and a Term,
And to the tripod ye would tie a lynx
110 That in his struggle throws the thyrsus down,
To comfort me on my entablature
Whereon I am to lie till I must ask
'Do I live, am I dead?' There, leave me, there!
For ye have stabbed me with ingratitude
115 To death – ye wish it – God, ye wish it! Stone –
Gritstone, a-crumble! Clammy squares which sweat
As if the corpse they keep were oozing through –
And no more *lapis* to delight the world!
Well go! I bless ye. Fewer tapers there,
120 But in a row: and, going, turn your backs
– Ay, like departing altar-ministrants,
And leave me in my church, the church for peace,
That I may watch at leisure if he leers –
Old Gandolf, at me, from his onion-stone,
125 As still he envied me, so fair she was!

The Laboratory

Ancien Régime

I

Now that I, tying thy glass mask tightly,
May gaze thro' these faint smokes curling whitely,
As thou pliest thy trade in this devil's-smithy –
Which is the poison to poison her, prithee?

II

He is with her, and they know that I know
Where they are, what they do: they believe my
      tears flow
While they laugh, laugh at me, at me fled to
      the drear
Empty church, to pray God in, for them! – I
      am here.

III

Grind away, moisten and mash up thy paste,
Pound at thy powder, – I am not in haste!
Better sit thus, and observe thy strange things,
Than go where men wait me and dance at
      the King's.

IV

That in the mortar – you call it a gum?
Ah, the brave tree whence such gold oozings come!
And yonder soft phial, the exquisite blue,
Sure to taste sweetly, – is that poison too?

V

Had I but all of them, thee and thy treasures,
What a wild crowd of invisible pleasures!
To carry pure death in an earring, a casket,
20   A signet, a fan-mount, a filigree basket!

VI

Soon, at the King's, a mere lozenge to give,
And Pauline should have just thirty minutes
        to live!
But to light a pastile, and Elise, with her head
And her breast and her arms and her hands
        should drop dead!

VII

25   Quick – is it finished? The colour's too grim!
Why not soft like the phial's, enticing and dim?
Let it brighten her drink, let her turn it and stir,
And try it and taste, ere she fix and prefer!

VIII

What a drop! She's not little, no minion like me!
30   That's why she ensnared him: this never will free
The soul from those masculine eyes, – say, 'no!'
To that pulse's magnificent come-and-go.

IX

For only last night, as they whispered, I brought
My own eyes to bear on her so, that I thought
35   Could I keep them one half minute fixed, she
        would fall
Shrivelled; she fell not; yet this does it all!

X

Not that I bid you spare her the pain;
Let death be felt and the proof remain:
Brand, burn up, bite into its grace –
40   He is sure to remember her dying face!

XI

Is it done? Take my mask off! Nay, be not morose;
It kills her, and this prevents seeing it close:
The delicate droplet, my whole fortune's fee!
If it hurts her, beside, can it ever hurt me?

XII

45   Now, take all my jewels, gorge gold to your fill,
You may kiss me, old man, on my mouth if
        you will!
But brush this dust off me, lest horror it brings
Ere I know it – next moment I dance at the King's!

Meeting at Night

I

The grey sea and the long black land;
And the yellow half-moon large and low;
And the startled little waves that leap
In fiery ringlets from their sleep,
5   As I gain the cove with pushing prow,
And quench its speed i' the slushy sand.

II

Then a mile of warm sea-scented beach;
Three fields to cross till a farm appears;
A tap at the pane, the quick sharp scratch
10   And blue spurt of a lighted match,
And a voice less loud, thro' its joys and fears,
Than the two hearts beating each to each!

Parting at Morning

Round the cape of a sudden came the sea,
And the sun looked over the mountain's rim:
And straight was a path of gold for him,
And the need of a world of men for me.

Love Among the Ruins

I

Where the quiet-coloured end of evening smiles,
    Miles and miles
On the solitary pastures where our sheep
    Half-asleep
5   Tinkle homeward thro' the twilight, stray or stop
    As they crop –
Was the site once of a city great and gay,
    (So they say)
Of our country's very capital, its prince
10   Ages since

Held his court in, gathered councils, wielding far
    Peace or war.

II

Now, – the country does not even boast a tree,
    As you see,
15   To distinguish slopes of verdure, certain rills
        From the hills
Intersect and give a name to, (else they run
    Into one)
Where the domed and daring palace shot its spires
20   Up like fires
O'er the hundred-gated circuit of a wall
    Bounding all,
Made of marble, men might march on nor be
       pressed,
    Twelve abreast.

III

25   And such plenty and perfection, see, of grass
      Never was!
Such a carpet as, this summer-time, o'erspreads
    And embeds
Every vestige of the city, guessed alone,
30   Stock or stone –
Where a multitude of men breathed joy and woe
    Long ago;
Lust of glory pricked their hearts up, dread of shame
    Struck them tame;
35   And that glory and that shame alike, the gold
    Bought and sold.

IV

Now, – the single little turret that remains
    On the plains,
By the caper overrooted, by the gourd
40   Overscored,
While the patching houseleek's head of blossom
      winks
    Through the chinks –
Marks the basement whence a tower in ancient time
    Sprang sublime,
45 And a burning ring, all round, the chariots traced
    As they raced,
And the monarch and his minions and his dames
    Viewed the games.

V

And I know, while thus the quiet-coloured eve
50   Smiles to leave
To their folding, all our many-tinkling fleece
    In such peace,
And the slopes and rills in undistinguished grey
    Melt away –
55 That a girl with eager eyes and yellow hair
    Waits me there
In the turret whence the charioteers caught soul
    For the goal,
When the king looked, where she looks now,
      breathless, dumb
60   Till I come.

VI

But he looked upon the city, every side,
    Far and wide,

All the mountains topped with temples, all the
    glades'
    Colonnades,
65   All the causeys, bridges, aqueducts, – and then
    All the men!
When I do come, she will speak not, she will stand,
    Either hand
On my shoulder, give her eyes the first embrace
70   Of my face,
Ere we rush, ere we extinguish sight and speech
    Each on each.

VII

In one year they sent a million fighters forth
    South and North,
75   And they built their gods a brazen pillar high
    As the sky,
Yet reserved a thousand chariots in full force –
    Gold, of course.
Oh heart! oh blood that freezes, blood that burns!
80   Earth's returns
For whole centuries of folly, noise and sin!
    Shut them in,
With their triumphs and their glories and the rest!
    Love is best.

Up at a Villa – Down in the City

(As Distinguished by an Italian Person of Quality)

I

Had I but plenty of money, money enough and to
  spare,
The house for me, no doubt, were a house in the
  city-square;
Ah, such a life, such a life, as one leads at the
  window there!

II

Something to see, by Bacchus, something to hear,
  at least!
There, the whole day long, one's life is a perfect
  feast;
While up at a villa one lives, I maintain it, no
  more than a beast.

III

Well now, look at our villa! stuck like the horn of
  a bull
Just on a mountain-edge as bare as the creature's
  skull,
Save a mere shag of a bush with hardly a leaf to
  pull!
– I scratch my own, sometimes, to see if the hair's
  turned wool.

IV

But the city, oh the city – the square with the
  houses! Why?

33

They are stone-faced, white as a curd, there's
    something to take the eye!
Houses in four straight lines, not a single front
    awry;
You watch who crosses and gossips, who saunters,
    who hurries by;
15   Green blinds, as a matter of course, to draw when
    the sun gets high;
And the shops with fanciful signs which are
    painted properly.

V

What of a villa? Though winter be over in March
    by rights,
'Tis May perhaps ere the snow shall have withered
    well off the heights:
You've the brown ploughed land before, where the
    oxen steam and wheeze,
20   And the hills over-smoked behind by the faint grey
    olive-trees.

VI

Is it better in May, I ask you? You've summer all at
    once;
In a day he leaps complete with a few strong April
    suns.
'Mid the sharp short emerald wheat, scarce risen
    three fingers well,
The wild tulip, at end of its tube, blows out its
    great red bell
25   Like a thin clear bubble of blood, for the children
    to pick and sell.

VII

Is it ever hot in the square? There's a fountain to
    spout and splash!
In the shade it sings and springs; in the shine such
    foam-bows flash
On the horses with curling fish-tails, that prance
    and paddle and pash
Round the lady atop in her conch fifty gazers do
    not abash,
30   Though all that she wears is some weeds round her
    waist in a sort of sash.

VIII

All the year long at the villa, nothing to see though
    you linger,
Except yon cypress that points like death's lean
    lifted forefinger.
Some think fireflies pretty, when they mix i' the
    corn and mingle,
Or thrid the stinking hemp till the stalks of it
    seem a-tingle.
35   Late August or early September, the stunning
    cicala is shrill,
And the bees keep their tiresome whine round the
    resinous firs on the hill.
Enough of the seasons, – I spare you the months
    of the fever and chill.

IX

Ere you open your eyes in the city, the blessed
    church-bells begin:
No sooner the bells leave off than the diligence
    rattles in:

40   You get the pick of the news, and it costs you
              never a pin.
       By-and-by there's the travelling doctor gives pills,
              lets blood, draws teeth;
       Or the Pulcinello-trumpet breaks up the market
              beneath.
       At the post-office such a scene-picture – the new
              play, piping hot!
       And a notice how, only this morning, three liberal
              thieves were shot.
45   Above it, behold the Archbishop's most fatherly
              of rebukes,
       And beneath, with his crown and his lion, some
              little new law of the Duke's!
       Or a sonnet with flowery marge, to the Reverend
              Don So-and-so
       Who is Dante, Boccaccio, Petrarca, Saint Jerome
              and Cicero,
       'And moreover,' (the sonnet goes rhyming,) 'the
              skirts of Saint Paul has reached,
50   Having preached us those six Lent-lectures more
              unctuous than ever he preached.'
       Noon strikes, – here sweeps the procession! our
              Lady borne smiling and smart
       With a pink gauze gown all spangles, and seven
              swords stuck in her heart!
       Bang-whang-whang goes the drum, *tootle-te-tootle*
              the fife;
       No keeping one's haunches still: it's the greatest
              pleasure in life.

X

55   But bless you, it's dear – it's dear! fowls, wine, at
              double the rate.
       They have clapped a new tax upon salt, and what

oil pays passing the gate

It's a horror to think of. And so, the villa for me,
  not the city!

Beggars can scarcely be choosers: but still – ah, the
  pity, the pity!

Look, two and two go the priests, then the monks
  with cowls and sandals,

60 And the penitents dressed in white shirts,
      a-holding the yellow candles;

One, he carries a flag up straight, and another a
  cross with handles,

And the Duke's guard brings up the rear, for the
  better prevention of scandals:

Bang-whang-whang goes the drum, *tootle-te-tootle*
  the fife.

Oh, a day in the city-square, there is no such
  pleasure in life!

A Woman's Last Word

Let's contend no more, Love
    Strive nor weep –
All be as before, Love,
    – Only sleep!

5   What so wild as words are?
        – I and thou
In debate, as birds are,
    Hawk on bough!

See the creature stalking
10   While we speak –
Hush and hide the talking,
    Cheek on cheek!

37

What so false as truth is,
    False to thee?
15   Where the serpent's tooth is,
    Shun the tree –

Where the apple reddens
    Never pry –
Lest we lose our Edens,
20   Eve and I!

Be a god and hold me
    With a charm –
Be a man and fold me
    With thine arm!

25   Teach me, only teach, Love!
    As I ought
I will speak thy speech, Love,
    Think thy thought –

Meet, if thou require it,
30   Both demands,
Laying flesh and spirit
    In thy hands!

That shall be to-morrow
    Not to-night:
35   I must bury sorrow
    Out of sight.

– Must a little weep, Love,
    – Foolish me!
And so fall asleep, Love,
40   Loved by thee.

Fra Lippo Lippi

I am poor brother Lippo, by your leave!
You need not clap your torches to my face.
Zooks, what's to blame? you think you see
    a monk!
What, 'tis past midnight, and you go the rounds,
5   And here you catch me at an alley's end
Where sportive ladies leave their doors ajar?
The Carmine's my cloister: hunt it up,
Do, – harry out, if you must show your zeal,
Whatever rat, there, haps on his wrong hole,
10   And nip each softling of a wee white mouse,
Weke, weke, that's crept to keep him company!
Aha, you know your betters! Then, you'll take
Your hand away that's fiddling on my throat,
And please to know me likewise. Who am I?
15   Why, one, sir, who is lodging with a friend
Three streets off – he's a certain... how
    d'ye call?
Master – a... Cosimo of the Medici,
I' the house that caps the corner. Boh! you
    were best!
Remember and tell me, the day you're hanged,
20   How you affected such a gullet's-gripe!
But you, sir, it concerns you that your knaves
Pick up a manner nor discredit you:
Zooks, are we pilchards, that they sweep the streets
And count fair prize what comes into their net?
25   He's Judas to a tittle, that man is!
Just such a face! Why, sir, you make amends.
Lord, I'm not angry! Bid your hangdogs go
Drink out this quarter-florin to the health
Of the munificent House that harbours me
30   (And many more beside, lads! more beside!)

And all's come square again. I'd like his face –
His, elbowing on his comrade in the door
With the pike and lantern, – for the slave
    that holds
John Baptist's head a-dangle by the hair
35   With one hand ('Look you, now,' as who
    should say)
And his weapon in the other, yet unwiped!
It's not your chance to have a bit of chalk,
A wood-coal or the like? or you should see!
Yes, I'm the painter, since you style me so.
40   What, brother Lippo's doings, up and down,
You know them and they take you? like enough!
I saw the proper twinkle in your eye –
'Tell you, I liked your looks at very first.
Let's sit and set things straight now, hip to haunch.
45   Here's spring come, and the nights one makes
    up bands
To roam the town and sing out carnival,
And I've been three weeks shut within my mew,
A-painting for the great man, saints and saints
And saints again. I could not paint all night –
50   Ouf! I leaned out of window for fresh air.
There came a hurry of feet and little feet,
A sweep of lute-strings, laughs, and whifts
    of song, –
Flower o' the broom,
Take away love, and our earth is a tomb!
55   *Flower o' the quince,*
I let Lisa go, and what good in life since?
Flower o' the thyme – and so on. Round they went.
Scarce had they turned the corner when a titter
Like the skipping of rabbits by moonlight, –
    three slim shapes,

60 And a face that looked up... zooks, sir, flesh and
blood,
That's all I'm made of! Into shreds it went,
Curtain and counterpane and coverlet,
All the bed-furniture – a dozen knots,
There was a ladder! Down I let myself,
65 Hands and feet, scrambling somehow, and so dropped,
And after them. I came up with the fun
Hard by Saint Laurence, hail fellow, well met, –
Flower o' the rose,
If I've been merry, what matter who knows?
70 And so as I was stealing back again
To get to bed and have a bit of sleep
Ere I rise up to-morrow and go work
On Jerome knocking at his poor old breast
With his great round stone to subdue the flesh,
75 You snap me of the sudden. Ah, I see!
Though your eye twinkles still, you shake
your head –
Mine's shaved – a monk, you say – the sting's
in that!
If Master Cosimo announced himself,
Mum's the word naturally; but a monk!
80 Come, what am I a beast for? tell us, now!
I was a baby when my mother died
And father died and left me in the street.
I starved there, God knows how, a year or two
On fig-skins, melon-parings, rinds and shucks,
85 Refuse and rubbish. One fine frosty day,
My stomach being empty as your hat,
The wind doubled me up and down I went.
Old Aunt Lapaccia trussed me with one hand,
(Its fellow was a stinger as I knew)
90 And so along the wall, over the bridge,
By the straight cut to the convent. Six words there,

While I stood munching my first bread that month:
'So, boy, you're minded,' quoth the good fat father
Wiping his own mouth, 'twas refection-time, –

95 'To quit this very miserable world?
Will you renounce'... 'the mouthful of bread?'
    thought I;
By no means! Brief, they made a monk of me;
I did renounce the world, its pride and greed,
Palace, farm, villa, shop and banking-house,

100 Trash, such as these poor devils of Medici
Have given their hearts to – all at eight years old.
Well, sir, I found in time, you may be sure,
'Twas not for nothing – the good bellyful,
The warm serge and the rope that goes all round,

105 And day-long blessed idleness beside!
'Let's see what the urchin's fit for' – that came next.
Not overmuch their way, I must confess.
Such a to-do! They tried me with their books:
Lord, they'd have taught me Latin in pure waste!

110 *Flower o' the clove,*
All the Latin I construe is, 'amo' I love!
But, mind you, when a boy starves in the streets
Eight years together, as my fortune was,
Watching folk's faces to know who will fling

115 The bit of half-stripped grape-bunch he desires,
And who will curse or kick him for his pains, –
Which gentleman processional and fine,
Holding a candle to the Sacrament,
Will wink and let him lift a plate and catch

120 The droppings of the wax to sell again,
Or holla for the Eight and have him whipped, –
How say I? – nay, which dog bites, which
    lets drop
His bone from the heap of offal in the street, –
Why, soul and sense of him grow sharp alike,

125 He learns the look of things, and none the less
For admonition from the hunger-pinch.
I had a store of such remarks, be sure,
Which, after I found leisure, turned to use.
I drew men's faces on my copy-books,

130 Scrawled them within the antiphonary's marge,
Joined legs and arms to the long music-notes,
Found eyes and nose and chin for A's and B's,
And made a string of pictures of the world
Betwixt the ins and outs of verb and noun,

135 On the wall, the bench, the door. The monks
      looked black.
'Nay,' quoth the Prior, 'turn him out, d'ye say?
In no wise. Lose a crow and catch a lark.
What if at last we get our man of parts,
We Carmelites, like those Camaldolese

140 And Preaching Friars, to do our church up fine
And put the front on it that ought to be!'
And hereupon he bade me daub away.
Thank you! my head being crammed, the walls
      a blank,
Never was such prompt disemburdening.

145 First, every sort of monk, the black and white,
I drew them, fat and lean: then, folk at church,
From good old gossips waiting to confess
Their cribs of barrel-droppings, candle-ends, –
To the breathless fellow at the altar-foot,

150 Fresh from his murder, safe and sitting there
With the little children round him in a row
Of admiration, half for his beard and half
For that white anger of his victim's son
Shaking a fist at him with one fierce arm,

155 Signing himself with the other because of Christ
(Whose sad face on the cross sees only this
After the passion of a thousand years)

Till some poor girl, her apron o'er her head,
(Which the intense eyes looked through) came
    at eve
160   On tiptoe, said a word, dropped in a loaf,
Her pair of earrings and a bunch of flowers
(The brute took growling), prayed, and so
    was gone.
I painted all, then cried ' 'Tis ask and have;
Choose, for more's ready!' – laid the ladder flat,
165   And showed my covered bit of cloister-wall.
The monks closed in a circle and praised loud
Till checked, taught what to see and not to see,
Being simple bodies, – 'That's the very man!
Look at the boy who stoops to pat the dog!
170   That woman's like the Prior's niece who comes
To care about his asthma: it's the life!'
But there my triumph's straw-fire flared and
    funked;
Their betters took their turn to see and say:
The Prior and the learned pulled a face
175   And stopped all that in no time. 'How?
    what's here?
Quite from the mark of painting, bless us all!
Faces, arms, legs and bodies like the true
As much as pea and pea! it's devil's-game!
Your business is not to catch men with show,
180   With homage to the perishable clay,
But lift them over it, ignore it all,
Make them forget there's such a thing as flesh.
Your business is to paint the souls of men –
Man's soul, and it's a fire, smoke... no, it's not...
185   It's vapour done up like a new-born babe –
(In that shape when you die it leaves your mouth)
It's... well, what matters talking, it's the soul!
Give us no more of body than shows soul!

Here's Giotto, with his Saint a-praising God,
190 That sets us praising, – why not stop with him?
Why put all thoughts of praise out of our head
With wonder at lines, colours, and what not?
Paint the soul, never mind the legs and arms!
Rub all out, try at it a second time.
195 Oh, that white smallish female with the breasts,
She's just my niece... Herodias, I would say, –
Who went and danced and got men's heads
          cut off!
Have it all out!' Now, is this sense, I ask?
A fine way to paint soul, by painting body
200 So ill, the eye can't stop there, must go further
And can't fare worse! Thus, yellow does for white
When what you put for yellow's simply black,
And any sort of meaning looks intense
When all beside itself means and looks nought.
205 Why can't a painter lift each foot in turn,
Left foot and right foot, go a double step,
Make his flesh liker and his soul more like,
Both in their order? Take the prettiest face,
The Prior's niece... patron-saint – is it so pretty
210 You can't discover if it means hope, fear,
Sorrow or joy? won't beauty go with these?
Suppose I've made her eyes all right and blue,
Can't I take breath and try to add life's flash,
And then add soul and heighten them threefold?
215 Or say there's beauty with no soul at all –
(I never saw it – put the case the same –)
If you get simple beauty and nought else,
You get about the best thing God invents:
That's somewhat: and you'll find the soul you
          have missed,
220 Within yourself, when you return him thanks.
'Rub all out!' Well, well, there's my life, in short,

And so the thing has gone on ever since.
I'm grown a man no doubt, I've broken bounds:
You should not take a fellow eight years old
225   And make him swear to never kiss the girls.
I'm my own master, paint now as I please –
Having a friend, you see, in the Corner-house!
Lord, it's fast holding by the rings in front –
Those great rings serve more purposes than just
230   To plant a flag in, or tie up a horse!
And yet the old schooling sticks, the old grave eyes
Are peeping o'er my shoulder as I work,
The heads shake still – 'It's art's decline, my son!
You're not of the true painters, great and old;
235   Brother Angelico's the man, you'll find;
Brother Lorenzo stands his single peer:
Fag on at flesh, you'll never make the third!'
Flower o' the pine,
You keep your mistr... manners, and I'll stick to mine!
240   I'm not the third, then: bless us, they must know!
Don't you think they're the likeliest to know,
They with their Latin? So, I swallow my rage,
Clench my teeth, suck my lips in tight, and paint
To please them – sometimes do and sometimes
        don't;
245   For, doing most, there's pretty sure to come
A turn, some warm eve finds me at my saints –
A laugh, a cry, the business of the world –
(*Flower o' the peach,*
Death for us all, and his own life for each!)
250   And my whole soul revolves, the cup runs over,
The world and life's too big to pass for a dream,
And I do these wild things in sheer despite,
And play the fooleries you catch me at,
In pure rage! The old mill-horse, out at grass
255   After hard years, throws up his stiff heels so,

Although the miller does not preach to him
The only good of grass is to make chaff.
What would men have? Do they like grass or no –
May they or mayn't they? all I want's the thing
260   Settled for ever one way. As it is,
You tell too many lies and hurt yourself:
You don't like what you only like too much,
You do like what, if given you at your word,
You find abundantly detestable.
265   For me, I think I speak as I was taught;
I always see the garden and God there
A-making man's wife: and, my lesson learned,
The value and significance of flesh,
I can't unlearn ten minutes afterwards.

270   You understand me: I'm a beast, I know.
But see, now – why, I see as certainly
As that the morning-star's about to shine,
What will hap some day. We've a youngster here
Comes to our convent, studies what I do,
275   Slouches and stares and lets no atom drop:
His name is Guidi – he'll not mind the monks –
They call him Hulking Tom, he lets them talk –
He picks my practice up – he'll paint apace,
I hope so – though I never live so long,
280   I know what's sure to follow. You be judge!
You speak no Latin more than I, belike;
However, you're my man, you've seen the world
– The beauty and the wonder and the power,
The shapes of things, their colours, lights and
        shades,
285   Changes, surprises, – and God made it all!
– For what? Do you feel thankful, ay or no,
For this fair town's face, yonder river's line,
The mountain round it and the sky above,

Much more the figures of man, woman, child,
290   These are the frame to? What's it all about?
To be passed over, despised? or dwelt upon,
Wondered at? oh, this last of course! – you say.
But why not do as well as say, – paint these
Just as they are, careless what comes of it?
295   God's works – paint anyone, and count it crime
To let a truth slip. Don't object, 'His works
Are here already; nature is complete:
Suppose you reproduce her – (which you can't)
There's no advantage! you must beat her, then.'
300   For, don't you mark? we're made so that we love
First when we see them painted, things we
          have passed
Perhaps a hundred times nor cared to see;
And so they are better, painted – better to us,
Which is the same thing. Art was given for that;
305   God uses us to help each other so,
Lending our minds out. Have you noticed, now,
Your cullion's hanging face? A bit of chalk,
And trust me but you should, though! How
          much more,
If I drew higher things with the same truth!
310   That were to take the Prior's pulpit-place,
Interpret God to all of you! Oh, oh,
It makes me mad to see what men shall do
And we in our graves! This world's no blot for us,
Nor blank; it means intensely, and means good:
315   To find its meaning is my meat and drink.
'Ay, but you don't so instigate to prayer!'
Strikes in the Prior: 'when your meaning's plain
It does not say to folk – remember matins,
Or, mind you fast next Friday!' Why, for this
320   What need of art at all? A skull and bones,
Two bits of stick nailed crosswise, or, what's best,

A bell to chime the hour with, does as well.
I painted a Saint Laurence six months since
At Prato, splashed the fresco in fine style:
325 'How looks my painting, now the scaffold's down?'
I ask a brother: 'Hugely,' he returns –
'Already not one phiz of your three slaves
Who turn the Deacon off his toasted side,
But's scratched and prodded to our heart's content,
330 The pious people have so eased their own
With coming to say prayers there in a rage:
We get on fast to see the bricks beneath.
Expect another job this time next year,
For pity and religion grow i' the crowd –
335 Your painting serves its purpose!' Hang the fools!

– That is – you'll not mistake an idle word
Spoke in a huff by a poor monk, God wot,
Tasting the air this spicy night which turns
The unaccustomed head like Chianti wine!
340 Oh, the church knows! don't misreport me, now!
It's natural a poor monk out of bounds
Should have his apt word to excuse himself:
And hearken how I plot to make amends.
I have bethought me: I shall paint a piece
345 ... There's for you! Give me six months, then go, see
Something in Sant' Ambrogio's! Bless the nuns!
They want a cast o' my office. I shall paint
God in the midst, Madonna and her babe,
Ringed by a bowery flowery angel-brood,
350 Lilies and vestments and white faces, sweet
As puff on puff of grated orris-root
When ladies crowd to Church at midsummer.
And then i' the front, of course a saint or two –
Saint John, because he saves the Florentines,
355 Saint Ambrose, who puts down in black and white

The convent's friends and gives them a long day,
And Job, I must have him there past mistake,
The man of Uz (and Us without the z,
Painters who need his patience). Well, all these
360   Secured at their devotion, up shall come
Out of a corner when you least expect,
As one by a dark stair into a great light,
Music and talking, who but Lippo! I! –
Mazed, motionless and moonstruck – I'm
        the man!
365   Back I shrink – what is this I see and hear?
I, caught up with my monk's-things by mistake,
My old serge gown and rope that goes all round,
I, in this presence, this pure company!
Where's a hole, where's a corner for escape?
370   Then steps a sweet angelic slip of a thing
Forward, puts out a soft palm – 'Not so fast!'
– Addresses the celestial presence, 'nay –
He made you and devised you, after all,
Though he's none of you! Could Saint John
        there draw –
375   His camel-hair make up a painting-brush?
We come to brother Lippo for all that,
Iste perfecit opus!' So, all smile –
I shuffle sideways with my blushing face
Under the cover of a hundred wings
380   Thrown like a spread of kirtles when you're gay
And play hot cockles, all the doors being shut,
Till, wholly unexpected, in there pops
The hothead husband! Thus I scuttle off
To some safe bench behind, not letting go
385   The palm of her, the little lily thing
That spoke the good word for me in the nick,
Like the Prior's niece... Saint Lucy, I would say.
And so all's saved for me, and for the church

390 A pretty picture gained. Go, six months hence!
Your hand, sir, and good-bye: no lights, no lights!
The street's hushed, and I know my own way back,
Don't fear me! There's the grey beginning. Zooks!

'Childe Roland to the Dark Tower Came'

(*See Edgar's song in Lear*)

I

My first thought was, he lied in every word,
　　That hoary cripple, with malicious eye
　　Askance to watch the working of his lie
On mine, and mouth scarce able to afford
5　Suppression of the glee, that pursed and scored
　　Its edge, at one more victim gained thereby.

II

What else should he be set for, with his staff?
　　What, save to waylay with his lies, ensnare
　　All travellers who might find him posted there,
10　And ask the road? I guessed what skull-like laugh
　　Would break, what crutch 'gin write my epitaph
　　For pastime in the dusty thoroughfare,

III

If at his counsel I should turn aside
　　Into that ominous tract which, all agree,
15　　Hides the Dark Tower. Yet acquiescingly
I did turn as he pointed: neither pride

Nor hope rekindling at the end descried,
    So much as gladness that some end might be.

IV

For, what with my whole world-wide wandering,
20   What with my search drawn out thro' years, my
        hope
    Dwindled into a ghost not fit to cope
With that obstreperous joy success would bring, –
I hardly tried now to rebuke the spring
    My heart made, finding failure in its scope.

V

25   As when a sick man very near to death
     Seems dead indeed, and feels begin and end
     The tears and takes the farewell of each friend,
And hears one bid the other go, draw breath
Freelier outside, ('since all is o'er,' he saith,
30   'And the blow fallen no grieving can amend;')

VI

While some discuss if near the other graves
     Be room enough for this, and when a day
     Suits best for carrying the corpse away,
With care about the banners, scarves and staves:
35   And still the man hears all, and only craves
     He may not shame such tender love and stay.

VII

Thus, I had so long suffered in this quest,
     Heard failure prophesied so oft, been writ
     So many times among 'The Band' – to wit,
40   The knights who to the Dark Tower's search
        addressed

Their steps – that just to fail as they, seemed best,
    And all the doubt was now – should I be fit?

VIII

So, quiet as despair, I turned from him,
    That hateful cripple, out of his highway
45   Into the path he pointed. All the day
Had been a dreary one at best, and dim
Was settling to its close, yet shot one grim
    Red leer to see the plain catch its estray.

IX

For mark! no sooner was I fairly found
50   Pledged to the plain, after a pace or two,
    Than, pausing to throw backward a last view
O'er the safe road, 'twas gone; grey plain
        all round:
Nothing but plain to the horizon's bound.
    I might go on; nought else remained to do.

X

55   So, on I went. I think I never saw
    Such starved ignoble nature; nothing throve:
    For flowers – as well expect a cedar grove!
But cockle, spurge, according to their law
Might propagate their kind, with none to awe,
60   You'd think; a burr had been a treasure-trove.

XI

No! penury, inertness and grimace,
    In some strange sort, were the land's portion.
      'See
    Or shut your eyes,' said Nature peevishly,
'It nothing skills: I cannot help my case:

65   'Tis the Last Judgment's fire must cure this place,
         Calcine its clods and set my prisoners free.'

XII

If there pushed any ragged thistle-stalk
    Above its mates, the head was chopped; the bents
    Were jealous else. What made those holes
        and rents
70 In the dock's harsh swarth leaves, bruised as to baulk
All hope of greenness? 'tis a brute must walk
    Pashing their life out, with a brute's intents.

XIII

As for the grass, it grew as scant as hair
    In leprosy; thin dry blades pricked the mud
75   Which underneath looked kneaded up with blood.
One stiff blind horse, his every bone a-stare,
Stood stupefied, however he came there:
    Thrust out past service from the devil's stud!

XIV

Alive? he might be dead for aught I know,
80   With that red gaunt and colloped neck a-strain,
    And shut eyes underneath the rusty mane;
Seldom went such grotesqueness with such woe;
I never saw a brute I hated so;
    He must be wicked to deserve such pain.

XV

85 I shut my eyes and turned them on my heart.
    As a man calls for wine before he fights,
        I asked one draught of earlier, happier sights,
Ere fitly I could hope to play my part.

Think first, fight afterwards – the soldier's art:
90   One taste of the old time sets all to rights.

XVI

Not it! I fancied Cuthbert's reddening face
        Beneath its garniture of curly gold,
        Dear fellow, till I almost felt him fold
An arm in mine to fix me to the place,
95   That way he used. Alas, one night's disgrace!
        Out went my heart's new fire and left it cold.

XVII

Giles then, the soul of honour – there he stands
        Frank as ten years ago when knighted first.
        What honest man should dare (he said) he durst.
100   Good – but the scene shifts – faugh! what hangman
                hands
Pin to his breast a parchment? His own bands
        Read it. Poor traitor, spit upon and curst!

XVIII

Better this present than a past like that;
        Back therefore to my darkening path again!
105   No sound, no sight as far as eye could strain.
Will the night send a howlet or a bat?
I asked: when something on the dismal flat
        Came to arrest my thoughts and change their
                train.

XIX

A sudden little river crossed my path
110   As unexpected as a serpent comes.
        No sluggish tide congenial to the glooms;
This, as it frothed by, might have been a bath

For the fiend's glowing hoof – to see the wrath
    Of its black eddy bespate with flakes and
        spumes.

XX

115 So petty yet so spiteful! All along,
    Low scrubby alders kneeled down over it;
    Drenched willows flung them headlong in a fit
Of mute despair, a suicidal throng:
The river which had done them all the wrong,
120   Whate'er that was, rolled by, deterred no whit.

XXI

Which, while I forded, – good saints, how I feared
    To set my foot upon a dead man's cheek,
    Each step, or feel the spear I thrust to seek
For hollows, tangled in his hair or beard!
125 – It may have been a water-rat I speared,
    But, ugh! it sounded like a baby's shriek.

XXII

Glad was I when I reached the other bank.
    Now for a better country. Vain presage!
    Who were the strugglers, what war did they wage,
130 Whose savage trample thus could pad the dank
Soil to a plash? Toads in a poisoned tank,
    Or wild cats in a red-hot iron cage –

XXIII

The fight must so have seemed in that fell cirque.
    What penned them there, with all the plain to
        choose?
135   No foot-print leading to that horrid mews,
None out of it. Mad brewage set to work

Their brains, no doubt, like galley-slaves the Turk
    Pits for his pastime, Christians against Jews.

XXIV

And more than that – a furlong on – why, there!
140   What bad use was that engine for, that wheel,
        Or brake, not wheel – that harrow fit to reel
Men's bodies out like silk? with all the air
Of Tophet's tool, on earth left unaware,
        Or brought to sharpen its rusty teeth of steel.

XXV

145 Then came a bit of stubbed ground, once a wood,
        Next a marsh, it would seem, and now mere earth
        Desperate and done with; (so a fool finds mirth,
Makes a thing and then mars it, till his mood
Changes and off he goes!) within a rood –
150   Bog, clay and rubble, sand and stark black dearth.

XXVI

Now blotches rankling, coloured gay and grim,
    Now patches where some leanness of the soil's
    Broke into moss or substances like boils;
Then came some palsied oak, a cleft in him
155 Like a distorted mouth that splits its rim
    Gaping at death, and dies while it recoils.

XXVII

And just as far as ever from the end!
    Nought in the distance but the evening, nought
    To point my footstep further! At the thought,
160 A great black bird, Apollyon's bosom-friend,
    Sailed past, nor beat his wide wing dragon-penned

That brushed my cap – perchance the guide I
sought.

XXVIII

For, looking up, aware I somehow grew,
   'Spite of the dusk, the plain had given place
165   All round to mountains – with such name to
       grace
Mere ugly heights and heaps now stolen in view.
How thus they had surprised me, – solve it, you!
How to get from them was no clearer case.

XXIX

Yet half I seemed to recognize some trick
170   Of mischief happened to me, God knows
       when –
In a bad dream perhaps. Here ended, then,
Progress this way. When, in the very nick
Of giving up, one time more, came a click
     As when a trap shuts – you're inside the den!

XXX

175 Burningly it came on me all at once,
     This was the place! those two hills on the right,
     Crouched like two bulls locked horn in horn in
       fight;
     While to the left, a tall scalped mountain... Dunce,
Dotard, a-dozing at the very nonce,
180   After a life spent training for the sight!

XXXI

What in the midst lay but the Tower itself?
     The round squat turret, blind as the fool's heart,
     Built of brown stone, without a counterpart

In the whole world. The tempest's mocking elf
185   Points to the shipman thus the unseen shelf
    He strikes on, only when the timbers start.

XXXII

Not see? because of night perhaps? — why, day
  Came back again for that! before it left,
  The dying sunset kindled through a cleft:
190   The hills, like giants at a hunting, lay,
  Chin upon hand, to see the game at bay, —
    'Now stab and end the creature — to the heft!'

XXXIII

Not hear? when noise was everywhere! it tolled
  Increasing like a bell. Names in my ears
195   Of all the lost adventurers my peers, —
How such a one was strong, and such was bold,
And such was fortunate, yet each of old
    Lost, lost! one moment knelled the woe of years.

XXXIV

There they stood, ranged along the hill-sides, met
200   To view the last of me, a living frame
  For one more picture! in a sheet of flame
I saw them and I knew them all. And yet
Dauntless the slug-horn to my lips I set,
    And blew. 'Childe Roland to the Dark Tower
      came.'

Love in a Life

I

Room after room,
I hunt the house through
We inhabit together.
Heart, fear nothing, for, heart, thou shalt find
    her –
5   Next time, herself! – not the trouble behind her
Left in the curtain, the couch's perfume!
As she brushed it, the cornice-wreath blossomed
    anew:
Yon looking-glass gleamed at the wave of her
    feather.

II

Yet the day wears,
10   And door succeeds door;
I try the fresh fortune –
Range the wide house from the wing to the centre.
Still the same chance! she goes out as I enter.
Spend my whole day in the quest, – who cares?
15   But 'tis twilight, you see, – with such suites to
    explore,
Such closets to search, such alcoves to importune!

Life in a Love

Escape me?
Never –
Beloved!
While I am I, and you are you,

5   So long as the world contains us both,
    Me the loving and you the loth,
While the one eludes, must the other pursue.
My life is a fault at last, I fear:
    It seems too much like a fate, indeed!
10   Though I do my best I shall scarce succeed.
But what if I fail of my purpose here?
It is but to keep the nerves at strain,
    To dry one's eyes and laugh at a fall,
And, baffled, get up and begin again, –
15   So the chace takes up one's life, that's all.
While, look but once from your farthest bound
    At me so deep in the dust and dark,
No sooner the old hope goes to ground
    Than a new one, straight to the self-same mark,
20 I shape me –
    Ever
    Removed!

The Last Ride Together

I

I said – Then, dearest, since 'tis so,
Since now at length my fate I know,
Since nothing all my love avails,
Since all my life seemed meant for, fails,
5   Since this was written and needs must be –
My whole heart rises up to bless
Your name in pride and thankfulness!
Take back the hope you gave, – I claim
Only a memory of the same,
10 – And this beside, if you will not blame,
    Your leave for one more last ride with me.

II

My mistress bent that brow of hers,
Those deep dark eyes where pride demurs
When pity would be softening through,
15   Fixed me a breathing-while or two
    With life or death in the balance – Right!
The blood replenished me again:
My last thought was at least not vain.
I and my mistress, side by side
20   Shall be together, breathe and ride,
So one day more am I deified.
    Who knows but the world may end to-night?

III

Hush! if you saw some western cloud
All billowy-bosomed, over-bowed
25   By many benedictions – sun's
And moon's and evening star's at once –
    And so, you, looking and loving best,
Conscious grew, your passion drew
Cloud, sunset, moonrise, star-shine too
30   Down on you, near and yet more near,
Till flesh must fade for heaven was here! –
Thus leant she and lingered – joy and fear!
    Thus lay she a moment on my breast.

IV

Then we began to ride. My soul
35   Smoothed itself out, a long-cramped scroll
Freshening and fluttering in the wind.
Past hopes already lay behind.
    What need to strive with a life awry?
Had I said that, had I done this,
40   So might I gain, so might I miss.

Might she have loved me? just as well
She might have hated, – who can tell?
Where had I been now if the worst befell?
    And here we are riding, she and I.

V

45   Fail I alone, in words and deeds?
    Why, all men strive and who succeeds?
    We rode; it seemed my spirit flew,
    Saw other regions, cities new,
        As the world rushed by on either side.
50   I thought, All labour, yet no less
    Bear up beneath their unsuccess.
    Look at the end of work, contrast
    The petty Done, the Undone vast,
    This present of theirs with the hopeful past!
55   I hoped she would love me. Here we ride.

VI

    What hand and brain went ever paired?
    What heart alike conceived and dared?
    What act proved all its thought had been?
    What will but felt the fleshly screen?
60   We ride and I see her bosom heave.
    There's many a crown for who can reach.
    Ten lines, a statesman's life in each!
    The flag stuck on a heap of bones,
    A soldier's doing! what atones?
65   They scratch his name on the Abbey-stones.
        My riding is better, by their leave.

VII

    What does it all mean, poet? Well,
    Your brains beat into rhythm, you tell

What we felt only; you expressed
70 You hold things beautiful the best,
   And pace them in rhyme so, side by side.
'Tis something, nay 'tis much: but then,
Have you yourself what's best for men?
Are you – poor, sick, old ere your time –
75 Nearer one whit your own sublime
Than we who never have turned a rhyme?
   Sing, riding's a joy! For me, I ride.

VIII

And you, great sculptor – so, you gave
A score of years to Art, her slave,
80 And that's your Venus, whence we turn
To yonder girl that fords the burn!
   You acquiesce, and shall I repine?
What, man of music, you grown grey
With notes and nothing else to say,
85 Is this your sole praise from a friend,
'Greatly his opera's strains intend,
But in music we know how fashions end!'
   I gave my youth; but we ride, in fine.

IX

Who knows what's fit for us? Had fate
90 Proposed bliss here should sublimate
My being – had I signed the bond –
Still one must lead some life beyond,
   Have a bliss to die with, dim-descried.
This foot once planted on the goal,
95 This glory-garland round my soul,
Could I descry such? Try and test!
I sink back shuddering from the quest.
Earth being so good, would heaven seem best?
   Now, heaven and she are beyond this ride.

X

100 And yet – she has not spoke so long!
What if heaven be that, fair and strong
At life's best, with our eyes upturned
Whither life's flower is first discerned,
  We, fixed so, ever should so abide?
105 What if we still ride on, we two
With life for ever old yet new,
Changed not in kind but in degree,
The instant made eternity, –
And heaven just prove that I and she
110 Ride, ride together, for ever ride?

The Patriot

An Old Story

I

It was roses, roses, all the way,
  With myrtle mixed in my path like mad;
The house-roofs seemed to heave and sway,
  The church-spires flamed, such flags they had,
5 A year ago on this very day.

II

The air broke into a mist with bells,
  The old walls rocked with the crowd and cries.
Had I said, 'Good folk, mere noise repels –
  But give me your sun from yonder skies!'
10 They had answered, 'And afterward, what else?'

III

Alack, it was I who leaped at the sun
    To give it my loving friends to keep!
Nought man could do, have I left undone:
    And you see my harvest, what I reap
15   This very day, now a year is run.

IV

There's nobody on the house-tops now –
    Just a palsied few at the windows set;
For the best of the sight is, all allow,
    At the Shambles' Gate – or, better yet,
20   By the very scaffold's foot, I trow.

V

I go in the rain, and, more than needs,
    A rope cuts both my wrists behind;
And I think, by the feel, my forehead bleeds,
    For they fling, whoever has a mind,
25   Stones at me for my year's misdeeds.

VI

Thus I entered, and thus I go!
    In triumphs, people have dropped down dead.
'Paid by the world, what dost thou owe
    Me?' – God might question; now instead,
30   'Tis God shall repay: I am safer so.

Andrea del Sarto

(Called 'The Faultless Painter')

But do not let us quarrel any more,
No, my Lucrezia; bear with me for once:
Sit down and all shall happen as you wish.
You turn your face, but does it bring your heart?
5   I'll work then for your friend's friend, never fear,
Treat his own subject after his own way,
Fix his own time, accept too his own price,
And shut the money into this small hand
When next it takes mine. Will it? tenderly?
10   Oh, I'll content him, – but to-morrow, Love!
I often am much wearier than you think,
This evening more than usual, and it seems
As if – forgive now – should you let me sit
Here by the window with your hand in mine
15   And look a half-hour forth on Fiesole,
Both of one mind, as married people use,
Quietly, quietly the evening through,
I might get up to-morrow to my work
Cheerful and fresh as ever. Let us try.
20   To-morrow, how you shall be glad for this!
Your soft hand is a woman of itself,
And mine the man's bared breast she curls inside.
Don't count the time lost, neither; you must serve
For each of the five pictures we require:
25   It saves a model. So! keep looking so –
My serpentining beauty, rounds on rounds!
– How could you ever prick those perfect ears,
Even to put the pearl there! oh, so sweet –
My face, my moon, my everybody's moon,
30   Which everybody looks on and calls his,
And, I suppose, is looked on by in turn,
While she looks – no one's: very dear, no less.

You smile? why, there's my picture ready made,
There's what we painters call our harmony!
A common greyness silvers everything, –
All in a twilight, you and I alike
– You, at the point of your first pride in me
(That's gone you know), – but I, at every point;
My youth, my hope, my art, being all toned down
To yonder sober pleasant Fiesole.
There's the bell clinking from the chapel-top;
That length of convent-wall across the way
Holds the trees safer, huddled more inside;
The last monk leaves the garden; days decrease,
And autumn grows, autumn in everything.
Eh? the whole seems to fall into a shape
As if I saw alike my work and self
And all that I was born to be and do,
A twilight-piece. Love, we are in God's hand.
How strange now, looks the life he makes us lead;
So free we seem, so fettered fast we are!
I feel he laid the fetter: let it lie!
This chamber for example – turn your head –
All that's behind us! You don't understand
Nor care to understand about my art,
But you can hear at least when people speak:
And that cartoon, the second from the door
– It is the thing, Love! so such things should be –
Behold Madonna! – I am bold to say.
I can do with my pencil what I know,
What I see, what at bottom of my heart
I wish for, if I ever wish so deep –
Do easily, too – when I say, perfectly,
I do not boast, perhaps: yourself are judge,
Who listened to the Legate's talk last week,
And just as much they used to say in France.
At any rate 'tis easy, all of it!

35

40

45

50

55

60

65

No sketches first, no studies, that's long past:
I do what many dream of, all their lives,
70   – Dream? strive to do, and agonize to do,
And fail in doing. I could count twenty such
On twice your fingers, and not leave this town,
Who strive – you don't know how the others
            strive
To paint a little thing like that you smeared
75   Carelessly passing with your robes afloat, –
Yet do much less, so much less, Someone says,
(I know his name, no matter) – so much less!
Well, less is more, Lucrezia: I am judged.
There burns a truer light of God in them,
80   In their vexed beating stuffed and stopped-up brain,
Heart, or whate'er else, than goes on to prompt
This low-pulsed forthright craftsman's hand of
            mine.
Their works drop groundward, but themselves,
            I know,
Reach many a time a heaven that's shut to me,
85   Enter and take their place there sure enough,
Though they come back and cannot tell the world.
My works are nearer heaven, but I sit here.
The sudden blood of these men! at a word –
Praise them, it boils, or blame them, it boils too.
90   I, painting from myself and to myself,
Know what I do, am unmoved by men's blame
Or their praise either. Somebody remarks
Morello's outline there is wrongly traced,
His hue mistaken; what of that? or else,
95   Rightly traced and well ordered; what of that?
Speak as they please, what does the mountain care?
Ah, but a man's reach should exceed his grasp,
Or what's a heaven for? All is silver-grey
Placid and perfect with my art: the worse!

100   I know both what I want and what might gain,
         And yet how profitless to know, to sigh
         'Had I been two, another and myself,
         Our head would have o'erlooked the world!'
            No doubt.
         Yonder's a work now, of that famous youth
105   The Urbinate who died five years ago.
         ('Tis copied, George Vasari sent it me.)
         Well, I can fancy how he did it all,
         Pouring his soul, with kings and popes to see,
         Reaching, that heaven might so replenish him,
110   Above and through his art – for it gives way;
         That arm is wrongly put – and there again –
         A fault to pardon in the drawing's lines,
         Its body, so to speak: its soul is right,
         He means right – that, a child may understand.
115   Still, what an arm! and I could alter it:
         But all the play, the insight and the stretch –
         Out of me, out of me! And wherefore out?
         Had you enjoined them on me, given me soul,
         We might have risen to Rafael, I and you!
120   Nay, Love, you did give all I asked, I think –
         More than I merit, yes, by many times.
         But had you – oh, with the same perfect brow,
         And perfect eyes, and more than perfect mouth,
         And the low voice my soul hears, as a bird
125   The fowler's pipe, and follows to the snare –
         Had you, with these the same, but brought a mind!
         Some women do so. Had the mouth there urged
         'God and the glory! never care for gain.
         The present by the future, what is that?
130   Live for fame, side by side with Agnolo!
         Rafael is waiting: up to God, all three!'
         I might have done it for you. So it seems:
         Perhaps not. All is as God over-rules.

Beside, incentives come from the soul's self;
135 The rest avail not. Why do I need you?
What wife had Rafael, or has Agnolo?
In this world, who can do a thing, will not;
And who would do it, cannot, I perceive:
Yet the will's somewhat – somewhat, too,
     the power –
140 And thus we half-men struggle. At the end,
God, I conclude, compensates, punishes.
'Tis safer for me, if the award be strict,
That I am something underrated here,
Poor this long while, despised, to speak the truth.
145 I dared not, do you know, leave home all day,
For fear of chancing on the Paris lords.
The best is when they pass and look aside;
But they speak sometimes; I must bear it all.
Well may they speak! That Francis, that first time,
150 And that long festal year at Fontainebleau!
I surely then could sometimes leave the ground,
Put on the glory, Rafael's daily wear,
In that humane great monarch's golden look, –
One finger in his beard or twisted curl
155 Over his mouth's good mark that made the smile,
One arm about my shoulder, round my neck,
The jingle of his gold chain in my ear,
I painting proudly with his breath on me,
All his court round him, seeing with his eyes,
160 Such frank French eyes, and such a fire of souls
Profuse, my hand kept plying by those hearts, –
And, best of all, this, this, this face beyond,
This in the background, waiting on my work,
To crown the issue with a last reward!
165 A good time, was it not, my kingly days?
And had you not grown restless... but I know –
'Tis done and past; 'twas right, my instinct said;

Too live the life grew, golden and not grey,
And I'm the weak-eyed bat no sun should tempt
170 Out of the grange whose four walls make his world.
How could it end in any other way?
You called me, and I came home to your heart.
The triumph was – to reach and stay there; since
I reached it ere the triumph, what is lost?
175 Let my hands frame your face in your hair's gold,
You beautiful Lucrezia that are mine!
'Rafael did this, Andrea painted that;
The Roman's is the better when you pray,
But still the other's Virgin was his wife – '
180 Men will excuse me. I am glad to judge
Both pictures in your presence; clearer grows
My better fortune, I resolve to think.
For, do you know, Lucrezia, as God lives,
Said one day Agnolo, his very self,
185 To Rafael... I have known it all these years...
(When the young man was flaming out his thoughts
Upon a palace-wall for Rome to see,
Too lifted up in heart because of it)
'Friend, there's a certain sorry little scrub
190 Goes up and down our Florence, none cares how,
Who, were he set to plan and execute
As you are, pricked on by your popes and kings,
Would bring the sweat into that brow of yours!'
To Rafael's! – And indeed the arm is wrong.
195 I hardly dare... yet, only you to see,
Give the chalk here – quick, thus the line should go!
Ay, but the soul! he's Rafael! rub it out!
Still, all I care for, if he spoke the truth,
(What he? why, who but Michael Agnolo?
200 Do you forget already words like those?)
If really there was such a chance, so lost, –
Is, whether you're – not grateful – but more pleased.

Well, let me think so. And you smile indeed!
This hour has been an hour! Another smile?
205 If you would sit thus by me every night
I should work better, do you comprehend?
I mean that I should earn more, give you more.
See, it is settled dusk now; there's a star;
Morello's gone, the watch-lights show the wall,
210 The cue-owls speak the name we call them by.
Come from the window, love, – come in, at last,
Inside the melancholy little house
We built to be so gay with. God is just.
King Francis may forgive me: oft at nights
215 When I look up from painting, eyes tired out,
The walls become illumined, brick from brick
Distinct, instead of mortar, fierce bright gold,
That gold of his I did cement them with!
Let us but love each other. Must you go?
220 That Cousin here again? he waits outside?
Must see you – you, and not with me? Those loans?
More gaming debts to pay? you smiled for that?
Well, let smiles buy me! have you more to spend?
While hand and eye and something of a heart
225 Are left me, work's my ware, and what's it worth?
I'll pay my fancy. Only let me sit
The grey remainder of the evening out,
Idle, you call it, and muse perfectly
How I could paint, were I but back in France,
230 One picture, just one more – the Virgin's face,
Not yours this time! I want you at my side
To hear them – that is, Michael Agnolo –
Judge all I do and tell you of its worth.
Will you? To-morrow, satisfy your friend.
235 I take the subjects for his corridor,
Finish the portrait out of hand – there, there,
And throw him in another thing or two

If he demurs; the whole should prove enough
To pay for this same Cousin's freak. Beside,
240   What's better and what's all I care about,
Get you the thirteen scudi for the ruff!
Love, does that please you? Ah, but what does he,
The Cousin! what does he to please you more?

I am grown peaceful as old age to-night.
245   I regret little, I would change still less.
Since there my past life lies, why alter it?
The very wrong to Francis! – it is true
I took his coin, was tempted and complied,
And built this house and sinned, and all is said.
250   My father and my mother died of want.
Well, had I riches of my own? you see
How one gets rich! Let each one bear his lot.
They were born poor, lived poor, and poor
      they died:
And I have laboured somewhat in my time
255   And not been paid profusely. Some good son
Paint my two hundred pictures – let him try!
No doubt, there's something strikes a balance. Yes,
You loved me quite enough, it seems to-night.
This must suffice me here. What would one have?
260   In heaven, perhaps, new chances, one more chance –
Four great walls in the New Jerusalem,
Meted on each side by the angel's reed,
For Leonard, Rafael, Agnolo and me
To cover – the three first without a wife,
265   While I have mine! So – still they overcome
Because there's still Lucrezia, – as I choose.

Again the Cousin's whistle! Go, my Love.

'De Gustibus – '

I

Your ghost will walk, you lover of trees,
   (If our loves remain)
   In an English lane,
By a cornfield-side a-flutter with poppies.
5   Hark, those two in the hazel coppice –
A boy and a girl, if the good fates please,
   Making love, say, –
   The happier they!
Draw yourself up from the light of the moon,
10   And let them pass, as they will too soon,
   With the bean-flowers' boon,
   And the blackbird's tune,
   And May, and June!

II

What I love best in all the world
15   Is a castle, precipice-encurled,
In a gash of the wind-grieved Apennine.
Or look for me, old fellow of mine,
   (If I get my head from out the mouth
O' the grave, and loose my spirit's bands,
20   And come again to the land of lands) –
In a sea-side house to the farther South,
Where the baked cicala dies of drouth,
And one sharp tree – 'tis a cypress – stands,
By the many hundred years red-rusted,
25   Rough iron-spiked, ripe fruit-o'ercrusted,
   My sentinel to guard the sands
   To the water's edge. For, what expands
Before the house, but the great opaque
Blue breadth of sea without a break?

30 While, in the house, for ever crumbles
    Some fragment of the frescoed walls,
    From blisters where a scorpion sprawls.
    A girl bare-footed brings, and tumbles
    Down on the pavement, green-flesh melons,
35 And says there's news to-day – the king
    Was shot at, touched in the liver-wing,
    Goes with his Bourbon arm in a sling:
    – She hopes they have not caught the felons.
    Italy, my Italy!
40 Queen Mary's saying serves for me –
        (When fortune's malice
        Lost her – Calais) –
    Open my heart and you will see
    Graved inside of it, 'Italy.'
45 Such lovers old are I and she:
    So it always was, so shall ever be!

Women and Roses

I

I dream of a red-rose tree.
And which of its roses three
Is the dearest rose to me?

II

Round and round, like a dance of snow
5   In a dazzling drift, as its guardians, go
    Floating the women faded for ages,
    Sculptured in stone, on the poet's pages.
    Then follow women fresh and gay,

Living and loving and loved to-day.
10 Last, in the rear, flee the multitude of maidens,
Beauties yet unborn. And all, to one cadence,
They circle their rose on my rose tree.

III

Dear rose, thy term is reached,
Thy leaf hangs loose and bleached:
15 Bees pass it unimpeached.

IV

Stay then, stoop, since I cannot climb,
You, great shapes of the antique time!
How shall I fix you, fire you, freeze you,
Break my heart at your feet to please you?
20 Oh, to possess and be possessed!
Hearts that beat 'neath each pallid breast!
Once but of love, the poesy, the passion,
Drink but once and die! – In vain, the same
          fashion,
They circle their rose on my rose tree.

V

25 Dear rose, thy joy's undimmed,
Thy cup is ruby-rimmed,
Thy cup's heart nectar-brimmed.

VI

Deep, as drops from a statue's plinth
The bee sucked in by the hyacinth,
30 So will I bury me while burning,
Quench like him at a plunge my yearning,
Eyes in your eyes, lips on your lips!
Fold me fast where the cincture slips,

Prison all my soul in eternities of pleasure,
35 Girdle me for once! But no – the old measure,
They circle their rose on my rose tree.

VII

Dear rose without a thorn,
Thy bud's the babe unborn:
First streak of a new morn.

VIII

40 Wings, lend wings for the cold, the clear!
What is far conquers what is near.
Roses will bloom nor want beholders,
Sprung from the dust where our flesh moulders.
What shall arrive with the cycle's change?
45 A novel grace and a beauty strange.
I will make an Eve, be the artist that began her,
Shaped her to his mind! – Alas! in like manner
They circle their rose on my rose tree.

Two in the Campagna

I

I wonder do you feel to-day
   As I have felt since, hand in hand,
We sat down on the grass, to stray
   In spirit better through the land,
5 This morn of Rome and May?

II

For me, I touched a thought, I know,
    Has tantalized me many times,
(Like turns of thread the spiders throw
    Mocking across our path) for rhymes
10   To catch at and let go.

III

Help me to hold it! First it left
    The yellowing fennel, run to seed
There, branching from the brickwork's cleft,
    Some old tomb's ruin: yonder weed
15   Took up the floating weft,

IV

Where one small orange cup amassed
    Five beetles, – blind and green they grope
Among the honey-meal: and last,
    Everywhere on the grassy slope
20   I traced it. Hold it fast!

V

The champaign with its endless fleece
    Of feathery grasses everywhere!
Silence and passion, joy and peace,
    An everlasting wash of air
25   Rome's ghost since her decease.

VI

Such life here, through such lengths of hours,
    Such miracles performed in play,
Such primal naked forms of flowers,

Such letting nature have her way
30   While heaven looks from its towers!

VII

How say you? Let us, O my dove,
    Let us be unashamed of soul,
As earth lies bare to heaven above!
    How is it under our control
35   To love or not to love?

VIII

I would that you were all to me,
    You that are just so much, no more.
Nor yours nor mine, nor slave nor free!
    Where does the fault lie? What the core
40   O' the wound, since wound must be?

IX

I would I could adopt your will,
    See with your eyes, and set my heart
Beating by yours, and drink my fill
    At your soul's springs, – your part my part
45   In life, for good and ill.

X

No. I yearn upward, touch you close,
    Then stand away. I kiss your cheek,
Catch your soul's warmth, – I pluck the rose
    And love it more than tongue can speak –
50   Then the good minute goes.

XI

Already how am I so far
  Out of that minute? Must I go
Still like the thistle-ball, no bar,
  Onward, whenever light winds blow,
55 Fixed by no friendly star?

XII

Just when I seemed about to learn!
  Where is the thread now? Off again!
The old trick! Only I discern –
  Infinite passion, and the pain
60 Of finite hearts that yearn.

Prospice

Fear death? – to feel the fog in my throat,
  The mist in my face,
When the snows begin, and the blasts denote
  I am nearing the place,
5 The power of the night, the press of the storm,
  The post of the foe;
Where he stands, the Arch Fear in a visible form,
  Yet the strong man must go:
For the journey is done and the summit attained,
10 And the barriers fall,
Though a battle's to fight ere the guerdon be
    gained,
  The reward of it all.
I was ever a fighter, so – one fight more,
  The best and the last!

15 I would hate that death bandaged my eyes, and
              forbore,
        And bade me creep past.
     No! let me taste the whole of it, fare like my peers
        The heroes of old,
     Bear the brunt, in a minute pay glad life's arrears
20   Of pain, darkness and cold.
     For sudden the worst turns the best to the brave,
        The black minute's at end,
     And the elements' rage, the fiend-voices that rave,
        Shall dwindle, shall blend,
25   Shall change, shall become first a peace out of pain,
        Then a light, then thy breast,
     O thou soul of my soul! I shall clasp thee again,
        And with God be the rest!

Apparent Failure

'We shall soon lose a celebrated building.'
                                    Paris Newspaper

I

No, for I'll save it! Seven years since,
   I passed through Paris, stopped a day
To see the baptism of your Prince;
   Saw, made my bow, and went my way:
5 Walking the heat and headache off,
   I took the Seine-side, you surmise,
Thought of the Congress, Gortschakoff,
   Cavour's appeal and Buol's replies,
So sauntered till – what met my eyes?

II

10 Only the Doric little Morgue!
    The dead-house where you show your drowned:
Petrarch's Vaucluse makes proud the Sorgue,
    Your Morgue has made the Seine renowned.
One pays one's debt in such a case;
15 I plucked up heart and entered, – stalked,
    Keeping a tolerable face
Compared with some whose cheeks were chalked:
    Let them! No Briton's to be baulked!

III

First came the silent gazers; next,
20   A screen of glass, we're thankful for;
Last, the sight's self, the sermon's text,
    The three men who did most abhor
Their life in Paris yesterday,
    So killed themselves: and now, enthroned
25 Each on his copper couch, they lay
    Fronting me, waiting to be owned.
I thought, and think, their sin's atoned.

IV

Poor men, God made, and all for that!
    The reverence struck me; o'er each head
30 Religiously was hung its hat,
    Each coat dripped by the owner's bed,
Sacred from touch: each had his berth,
    His bounds, his proper place of rest,
Who last night tenanted on earth
35   Some arch, where twelve such slept abreast,–
Unless the plain asphalte seemed best.

V

How did it happen, my poor boy?
    You wanted to be Buonaparte
And have the Tuileries for toy,
    40   And could not, so it broke your heart?
You, old one by his side, I judge,
    Were, red as blood, a socialist,
A leveller! Does the Empire grudge
    You've gained what no Republic missed?
45   Be quiet, and unclench your fist!

VI

And this – why, he was red in vain,
    Or black, – poor fellow that is blue!
What fancy was it turned your brain?
    Oh, women were the prize for you!
50   Money gets women, cards and dice
    Get money, and ill-luck gets just
The copper couch and one clear nice
    Cool squirt of water o'er your bust,
The right thing to extinguish lust!

VII

55   It's wiser being good than bad;
    It's safer being meek than fierce:
It's fitter being sane than mad.
    My own hope is, a sun will pierce
The thickest cloud earth ever stretched;
60   That, after Last, returns the First,
Though a wide compass round be fetched;
    That what began best, can't end worst,
Nor what God blessed once, prove accurst.

Notes

My Last Duchess

This is perhaps the most famous of Browning's poems, and it draws on his interests in Italy, Renaissance art and the use of the dramatic monologue. In this form of poetry there is a speaker, an implied audience, a past story and some implied present action. Note the use of rhyming couplets in this poem.

The character speaking in this monologue is based on the sixteenth-century Duke of Ferrara, who was enormously wealthy and married several times. His first wife died at the age of 17 in mysterious circumstances. The background situation in the poem is that the widowed Duke is in negotiations with an unnamed Count for his daughter's hand in marriage. Browning draws a sharp contrast between the Duke's aesthetic appreciation of art, and his murderous cruelty.

Four people are involved in the story related by the poem: the speaker (the Duke); the listener (the representative of the Count, who is alluded to in line 49); the speaker's late wife (depicted in the painting); and Frà Pandolf, the painter of her portrait. The Duke keeps a curtain drawn in front of the painting, and allows no one else to draw it aside.

1 The tone is matter-of-fact as the Duke reveals the painting to the visitor. Does this suggest that he feels no loss or pain at her passing? The reference to *my last Duchess* suggests that he sees her not as an individual but merely as one whose position in life was to be his Duchess – note the use of the possessive pronoun *my*.
   painted on the wall The portrait is a fresco, a painting made on the wet plaster of a wall.
2 **Looking as if she were alive** The dispassionate way in which he speaks about the painting serves to distance him again from any feelings about her death.
3 **Frà Pandolf** The painter of the fresco; a name made up by Browning. *Frà* means 'Brother', implying that the painter was a monk.

8　The Duke acknowledges the emotion depicted, but he distances himself from the subject of the painting by referring to her as *it*.

12　**such a glance**　Do we detect disapproval in this phrase?

14　**Her husband**　Again he distances himself from his connection with her by referring to himself in the third person.

14–15　**spot/ Of joy**　Notice the striking use of enjambment here. What do you make of this phrase (repeated in line 21)?

16–19　The assumptions that the Duke makes here about the conversation that might have passed between his wife and the painter suggest that he has given this great thought; clearly his wife's interaction with other people has been a preoccupation with him. However, phrases such as *such stuff* create a dismissive tone.

16　**mantle**　cloak.

21–34　**She had... With anybody's gift**　These lines develop the Duchess's character and, while the Duke is explaining what he disapproves of in her behaviour, they make her seem more appealing to the reader. The description of her as *too soon made glad,/ Too easily impressed* suggests excess, or at best a lack of discrimination, but these are nevertheless attractive characteristics, especially in contrast to those we can see in the Duke. His use of the disparaging term *officious fool* (line 27) reveals that he also disapproves of people who sought to please her.

25　**favour**　ribbon or badge indicating loyalty, traditionally given by a knight to a lady.

31–4　**She thanked... With anybody's gift**　The fragmented sentence structure in these lines reflects the irritation and anger that seem to bubble beneath his words. The adjectival compound used in the phrase *nine-hundred-years-old name* reinforces his conceit and arrogance by its very length, and serves to explain why he feels so affronted by the gratitude she shows to others.

34–5　**Who'd stoop to blame/ This sort of trifling?**　The rhetorical question reinforces the impression of the Duke as haughty and self-important. The words *stooping* and *stoop* are repeated in lines 42–3, suggesting his horror at the idea of lowering himself.

36　**(which I have not)**　Is this false modesty, given that the poem is full of evidence of the Duke's *skill/ In speech*? The

    phrase is counterbalanced in the same line by the notion of
    imposing his *will*.

40 **lessoned**   The relationship here appears to be one of pupil
    and teacher rather than husband and wife.

43–6 **smiled... smile... smiles**   This repetition seems to suggest an
    obsession, and it reaches a chilling climax in *Then all smiles*
    stopped together. What do you understand by this phrase?
    Late in life, when asked about this, Browning said that he
    had intended it to mean 'the commands were that she be put
    to death... Or he might have had her shut up in a convent'.

47 **As if alive**   This reprise of line 2 suggests that the Duke
    enjoys his complete control over the woman – she can be
    imagined to be alive, but now she is fixed for his gaze and
    he can control all access to the sight of her beauty.
    Will't please you rise?   The tone becomes polite and con-
    versational as the Duke turns his attentions to his visitor
    and the plans for the future marriage.

49 **munificence**   generosity.

50 **warrant**   guarantee.

51 **dowry**   payment made to the husband by the wife's family
    on marriage. Putting this issue before the mention of *his fair*
    daughter's self in the following line demonstrates clearly
    where the Duke's priorities lie, despite his claims to the
    contrary.

54–6 **Notice Neptune... cast in bronze for me**   The poem con-
    cludes with an image of a man who values the rarity and
    the containing power of art above personal relationships.
    What do you make of the subject that Browning uses for
    the bronze sculpture, *Neptune... Taming a sea-horse*?

56 **Claus of Innsbruck**   a fictional sculptor.

Porphyria's Lover

This poem first appeared as 'Porphyria' in the *Monthly Repository*
in January 1836, and is one of the first dramatic monologues
Browning wrote. This poem has a male speaker, who relates how
he was loved by a woman of a higher class than himself,
Porphyria. The narrator shockingly reveals how he has killed his
lover by strangling her with her own hair.

The speaker, or more accurately the thinker of the poem (the story is retold in the narrator's mind) is in his cottage after nightfall. Porphyria comes in from a raging storm and makes a fire, bringing cheer and warmth to the cottage. The sensual description of her embrace of the narrator as she offers him her bare shoulder reveals a passion and desire not commonly explored in Victorian poetry. It is made clear that this is an illicit relationship, and that Porphyria has other *ties* (line 24), although she is presented as the one who worships the narrator. His response to this devotion is to regard her as a possession, one that he fears to lose; to prevent this, he kills her, hoping to preserve the moment of intimacy. The poem concludes with the narrator questioning the response of God to his deed.

1–2   The use of the pathetic fallacy (where the weather reflects human emotions) in these opening lines creates an immediate atmosphere of turbulence. The wind is personified as *sullen*, and reflects the troubled state of mind of the speaker.

4   **vex**   annoy, trouble. This, together with *spite* in line 3, suggests anger and creates an atmosphere of discomfort.

6   **glided**   Porphyria's actions, by contrast, seem smooth, gentle, almost ghostly.

8   **cheerless grate**   empty hearth.

9   **Blaze up**   Literally, it is the fire in the hearth that blazes, but these words are also linked to the idea of human passion.

11–20   The details of Porphyria discarding her wet cloak, shawl and gloves, and loosening her hair, imply trust and intimacy. The verbs *Withdrew*, *laid… by*, and *let… fall* have sexual overtones. The atmosphere is transformed by her actions into one that is seductive and sensual.

22–5   The atmosphere changes again as the speaker offers his harsh judgement, referring to Porphyria's *pride*, the *vainer ties* she will not sacrifice for him, and his insecurity because she will not give herself to him *for ever*. What might the *vainer ties* consist of?

24   **dissever**   separate, break.

26   **But**   Does this word signal a further shift in attitude?

27 **to-night's gay feast** This gives a hint of all that Porphyria must leave behind if she is to be with her lover.
    restrain prevent.

29 **all in vain** all for nothing.

30 **So** Using this word to preface the reminder about the weather that Porphyria has braved implies a calculated rather than spontaneous reaction to her efforts to visit and comfort him.

33 **worshipped me** Note the suggestion of almost religious devotion.
    surprise Is this an unexpected reaction in the light of his earlier description of her passion and devotion?

35 **I debated what to do** Again there is a calculating response to Porphyria's revelation of her devotion.

36–7 **she was mine, mine, fair,/ Perfectly pure and good** The repetition of the possessive pronoun *mine* suggests obsession. The adjective *pure*, and the alliteration, create a sense of his pleasure at her being untainted, reinforced by *good*, suggesting virtue. The caesura (break in the line) after *good*, however, signals the end for Porphyria.

37–8 **I found/ A thing to do** The matter-of-fact coldness of this phrase echoes the calculating tone seen earlier in the poem and foreshadows the chilling detail the speaker offers about the manner of her death. What is the effect of positioning the phrase *A thing* at the beginning of a line?

38–41 **and all her hair... strangled her** The length of this description is noteworthy, as it winds through three lines, using enjambment – suggesting the three windings of Porphyria's hair. The brief phrase *And strangled her* contrasts with the attention drawn to her hair and throat.

42 This line creates a sense of the speaker's (insane?) complacency and arrogance.

43–4 **As a shut bud... her lids** This simile, and his action in opening her eyelids, are both particularly unsettling. On the one hand the potential sting of the *bee*, presumably present in the power of her eyes, has been contained by the speaker, though he is still wary of it. On the other hand the *bud* and *bee* suggest pollination and the burgeoning of life – but this has been snuffed out by the speaker.

45 This macabre image of her eyes, laughing and stainless, echoes the speaker's earlier anxiety; it seems that it is only now

she is dead that she is above jealousy and suspicion.

46 **tress** The fatal *long yellow string* (line 39) of hair has now become an innocent *tress*.

48 The alliterative 'b' sounds in this line reinforce the horror of his disquieting behaviour – he interprets the flush of blood returning to her face as a blush in response to his kiss.

50–51 **this time my shoulder bore/ Her head** The insistence on this reversal of roles (see line 19) implies the speaker's pride in his dominance. He is now active while she has become definitively passive.

51 **droops upon it still** Note the change to the present tense, and the insistence with the word *still* – and also *now* in line 58 – on the immediacy of the scene.

52 **smiling rosy little head** Porphyria is reduced, by these three adjectives, to near childishness. What is the effect of the repetition of *head*, and the related references to *it* and *its*, in the following lines? What has Porphyria become?

53 The speaker claims that his actions have given Porphyria the chance to satisfy her *utmost will* – to belong to him completely.

57 **Her darling one wish** Again, the speaker claims he knows what Porphyria truly desired, and has given it to her.

58–60 The lines that conclude the poem show the speaker not only assuming the right to interpret Porphyria's *will*, but believing that his deed could be approved by God.

Pictor Ignotus

Pictor Ignotus is Latin for 'unknown painter', a note that Browning would have seen written in art catalogues or on gallery labels when he was looking at Renaissance art. This dramatic monologue begins abruptly, with the speaker's claim that he could have painted in the style of the *youth* whose work is evidently admired by the 'you' of the poem. This *youth* is usually understood to be the celebrated and influential painter Raphael, who lived from 1483 to 1520. The ideas in this poem are in some ways similar to those in *Andrea del Sarto* (see page 67), in which Raphael is referred to as *that famous youth/ The Urbinate* (lines 104–5). Like *Andrea del Sarto* it is a psychological study of a man who is incapable of making full use of his talents, but is at the same time keenly aware of what he might have been, in contrast to what he is.

Implicit throughout this monologue is the sense of the paint-er's failure, both as an artist and as a human being. Browning's main inspiration for this poem, like many others, probably came from Giorgio Vasari's famous work, *Lives of the Most Excellent Painters, Sculptors and Architects* (1568), and in particular Vasari's description of the life of the painter known as Fra Bartolommeo. According to Vasari this painter spent a great deal of time in the company of Raphael, and Raphael was keen to emulate his man-ner of colouring. However, Fra Bartolommeo renounced paint-ing for a time and became a monk ('Fra' means 'Brother'). In this dramatic monologue, Browning presents the reader with an image of what a man such as Fra Bartolommeo may have been like, stressing his timidity and portraying him as considering *heaven* and worldly success as two mutually exclusive ambitions. Thus, as in *Andrea del Sarto*, Browning creates a speaker who can be regarded as a failure because he has retreated from life and failed to use the gifts he has been given.

3 **thought which saddens while it soothes** The fusion of these two opposing emotions reflects the complexity of the speaker's emotions as he considers what may have been achieved.

5–6 **all my gift/ Of fires from God** The image of *fires* suggest the magnificence and beauty of his ability to use colour powerfully to paint human passions.

6–8 **nor would my flesh... wide to heaven** Here the speaker suggests that his soul would not have been compromised in the pursuit of art, as he looks to heaven and the gift given from God.

11 The counter-balanced images of *licence* with *limit*, and *space* with *bound*, suggest on the one hand the idea of the bound-less possibilities of the imagination, but on the other hand constraint and containment. All this, he suggests, can be seen in humankind.

13–14 There is a tone of confidence or even arrogance here as the speaker flirts with the idea that he could have painted as well as anyone.

15–22 These lines describe the beauty and the realism of work created by newly emerging artists such as the much-praised Raphael; interestingly *Hope, Rapture* and *Confidence* are all capitalized as personifications, to focus the reader on the ways in which these abstract emotions or *passions* have been given life through the skill of painters. Lines 19–20 associate *Rapture* with the natural joy of the mother bird suckling her young. In contrast, *Confidence* is presented through an image of an uplifted forehead and a mouth that is *locked… fast*, shut up like a well-fortified *castle*.

23–4 The rhetorical questions here suggest a self-questioning that is explored in the following lines.

25–35 The speaker acknowledges that he has had moments of yearning for the fame such pictures as he has described would have brought him. Does the final image of *youth* such as Raphael *learning at my feet* (35), uttered as an exclamation, present us with a man who appears self-deluded, and jealous of the glory given to the bright new stars of Renaissance painting? Or were his dreams honourable ones?

36–40 Here the speaker continues to describe how he used to dream of achieving celebrity, *Here on my earth, earth's every man my friend*. He seems to long for that *love* and *praise* he imagines receiving. However, there is a jarring note as he alludes to failing to *go to heaven*, and it is this thought that acts as a catalyst to his rejection of worldly success, as he comes to acknowledge that his ambition was *so wildly dear*. What kind of character do you feel is being revealed to the reader at this point?

41 **But a voice changed it** The poem turns on these words, as the voice (is it only in his head?) leads him to question his ambitious desires, and seems to precipitate a crisis.

45–7 **Mixed with… judge me?** The world is changed for him, and what he now describes seems like a nightmare vision in which he is judged by the *cold faces* of those who commission and purchase works of art.

47–9 The image of him *Shrinking, as from the soldiery a nun* reveals his timidity and vulnerability and, one might almost argue, his innocence. The exclamation *enough!* implies finality, and signals that the speaker's change of mind is complete.

50–56 The mood of the speaker is now one of disgust, as he

describes the commercial aspects of the life of a painter at the mercy of the trivial judgements and vacillating moods of his patrons. They treat art as mere *household-stuff* and judge work in terms of their own personal *pettiness*.

57 **I chose my portion**   With this statement the painter rationalizes, to his own satisfaction, his rejection of the pursuit of worldly success.

58 The earlier descriptions of the joys of creating successful works of art are now counterbalanced by the reality that can make his heart sink. The word *monotonous* characterizes the repetitive and tedious work he is now engaged in.

59–64 Notice the subtle positives as well as the negative terms in these lines. That which is *endless* is also *eternal* (59), and the painter's subjects have a *cold calm beautiful regard*. The negation of passion fired by the imagination is emphasized by the words *cold* and *calm*, but the results are nevertheless *beautiful*. A further compensation is implied in the image of the *sanctuary's gloom* (63) – despite the *gloom*, he values the protection afforded by the *sanctuary*.

60 **the same series, Virgin, Babe and Saint**   Contrast the terms used here, describing more traditional works of art that are concerned with religious symbolism rather than human realism, with lines 15–16.

66–9 The mood is bleak here as the imagery is of death and decay. The speaker faces the reality of what will happen to his life's work: neglect and the passage of time ensure that it will *gently die*. How do you feel the presentation of the character has changed as we come to the end of the poem?

67 **travertine**   limestone.

70–72 The concluding rhetorical questions addressed to the successful *youth* seem to sum up the speaker's justification for his failure, and his rejection of worldly values. Ironically it has been his inability to see the value in the *specks of earth* that has resulted in his withdrawal from the world, and his attempt to maintain the moral high ground suggests that he is unable to accept the truth about his own limitations. How do you feel this poem links with *Andrea del Sarto* (page 67) and *Fra Lippo Lippi* (page 39)?

The Lost Leader

This is one of Browning's most personal poems, and it contains an attack on William Wordsworth (1770–1850), who is characterized as a *Lost Leader*. The celebrated Lakeland poet was politically radical in his youth but became increasingly conservative, took up a civil service post and government pension, and ultimately accepted the position of Poet Laureate in 1843 on the death of Robert Southey.

It is interesting to question why Browning should feel moved to make such a strong attack on an ageing poet who had said to him at a dinner a few years before that he was 'proud to drink your health, Mr Browning'. However, Browning had very decided liberal principles and a lifelong hatred of those whom he considered to be turncoats and traitors. The poem can also be read as a political one in which the speaker vilifies any leader who has compromised his principles and embraced the values of the ruling elite.

1 The image of a *handful of silver* conjures images of Judas Iscariot's betrayal of Christ for 'thirty pieces of silver'.

2 **riband** decoration signifying an official position, in this case that of Poet Laureate.

3–4 The paradox in these lines suggests that *fortune*, normally associated with good luck and prosperity, has in fact deprived the world of the poet's talents as all his gifts are now lost, to be replaced by official respectability.

5 The contrast created between *gold* and *silver* suggests the limitations of the rewards the poet has been offered by those in power. It alludes to issues of class and hierarchy and the subservient place of the artist, who remains at the mercy of those who will buy him and use his skills for their own ends. What link can you make here to *Pictor Ignotus* (page 17)?

7 The idea of class is reinforced through the image of *copper*, a base metal used for low-value coins, which Browning uses as a synecdoche to represent the devotion ordinary people felt for the poet, people such as those Wordsworth had celebrated in his ground-breaking work *Lyrical Ballads*.

8 The contrast between *Rags* and the colour *purple* illustrates the speaker's contempt for the robes of office; purple is a colour associated with the ruling classes and often worn by officials on state occasions.

9–12 The lamenting tone of these lines suggests the depth of emotion and the feelings of loss the speaker experiences. He presents himself and others like him modelling themselves on Wordsworth's attitudes, values and style of writing.

13–14 Citing these great writers and poets serves to isolate Wordsworth and to reinforce the sense of betrayal with which the poem began.

15–16 The idea of betrayal is strengthened by the use of the words *breaks* and *sinks* to describe the actions of the poet, who is seen to be a traitor to the *van* (vanguard, or leaders of a movement) and the *freemen* as he descends to the level of a *slave*.

17 The first part of this divided line has an optimistic and celebratory tone, but after the caesura the tone changes to one of contempt, and this is echoed in line 18.

18 **lyre**   musical instrument associated with the reciting of poetry.

19 **quiescence**   acquiescence, agreement.

21 **record one lost soul more**   How would you describe Browning's tone here? Is it bitter, dismissive, resigned, sad?

22–4 The repetition of *one more* emphasizes that many other losses have been suffered, and Browning uses religious imagery as he refers to the *sorrow* of *angels* in contrast to the *triumph* of *devils*. These lines seem to echo the sentiments expressed by John Milton in *Paradise Lost*, as pathos is created for the fall of one so great.

29–30 Interestingly, in these lines Browning appears to suggest that it is better for the leader who is now lost to *fight on* and follow his wrongful course rather than weakly return to those he has so openly betrayed; as argued in the preceding lines, they would never be able to trust him again.

31–2 The conclusion offers a surprising change in tone as the speaker appears to offer the possibility of reconciliation after the *fight* described in previous lines. The final image is of Wordsworth being received into *heaven* and being *Pardoned* as a result of finally being awakened to the *new knowledge*, and therefore deserving his position of *first by the throne*. What links can you make to *The Patriot* (page 65)?

Home-Thoughts, from Abroad

This is a poem that celebrates the beauty and freshness of England in springtime. In a similar vein to '*De Gustibus –*' (page 75), Browning uses visual and aural imagery to induce the reader to see and hear his subject matter. In a letter, Browning said his aim was to write poems 'with more music and painting... so as to get people to hear and see'. The speaker of this poem is cast in the role of the homesick traveller, and he describes a typical springtime scene in the countryside.

The form of this poem is unusual, as it divides into two stanzas of different forms with differing tones. The first stanza has a metrical pattern that suggests a rising and falling, which seem to reflect the emotional temperature of the speaker; in a positive mood he thinks of home, but then has to resign himself to the fact that he is many miles away. The rhythm and rhyme scheme of the longer second stanza give a more reflective mood to the poem, as the speaker considers the development of the seasons. The poem concludes in quite a surprising way, as the speaker appears to be dismissive of his present surroundings.

4   The fragmented sentence structure in this line slows the pace and serves to create a sense of the enduring surprise of the ever-changing English landscape. The word *unaware* suggests the subtle way in which spring in England arrives gradually and as if unexpectedly, as the seasons alter unannounced.

5–6   **boughs, brushwood sheaf, elm-tree bole**   The detailed, concrete images and alliteration offer vivid pictures of the subtle yet striking appearance of spring. The *bole* is the trunk or main stem of a tree.

7   The visual imagery is complemented by the sound of the chaffinch's song.

8   The final line of the stanza is punctuated by a dash, which forms a caesura or pause. This focuses the reader onto the immediacy of the moment, as if the images described have been caught in a time frame created through the use of the word *now*.

10   The activity of the birds links back to the first stanza and is used to characterize the movement of the seasons.

11–14   The statement *Hark I* (reversing normal word order) remains initially unexplained, as the speaker uses visual images invoked by the personification of the *blossomed pear tree*. It *Leans* and *scatters*, showering its *Blossoms* and *dewdrops*, providing a contrast with the green of the field and the clover. It is not until line 14 that the speaker returns to the allusion to hearing, as the *song* of the *wise thrush* is evoked.

14–16   **he sings... careless rapture!**   The description of the song being produced *twice over* is vividly reprised by the echoing of *recapture* and *rapture*; the complexity of the alliteration and feminine rhyme (in which the final syllable is unstressed) suggests the complexity and harmony of the song sequence.

17   **rough with hoary dew**   This provides a visual image of the early-morning, silvery dew that characterizes springtime in England.

19   **the little children's dower**   This image suggests the *buttercups* are nature's gift to children.

20   The mood changes in this last line as the speaker contrasts the glory of England with the inferior beauty of the *melon-flower*, which is clearly Mediterranean. It is described as *gaudy*, a word that suggests something that is showy, extremely colourful and possibly vulgar.

The Bishop Orders His Tomb at Saint Praxed's Church

This poem is another of Browning's dramatic monologues, and here he adopts the form of blank verse, with its iambic pentameter rhythm. Traditionally this was the form used by dramatists, and Browning adapts it to create the Bishop's voice – he is an earthy, straightforward man who does not try to be eloquent. A recent editor of Browning's works comments that 'Character portrayal by means of monologue has never been done with greater vividness than in this poem' (*Thirty Poems by Robert Browning*, ed. W.S. Mackie).

The poem is set in Renaissance Italy, where the dying Bishop is attempting to leave instructions for the design of his tomb within the church. Although the characters in the poem are imagined, the church is real and Browning visited it in Rome (where it is known as Santa Prassede, see page 186). Saint Praxed was a virgin saint, believed to be the daughter of a Roman centurion in the first century CE.

1   This opening line refers to Ecclesiastes 1:2, a biblical warning about the emptiness or futility of life.

2   **Draw round**   The imperative voice immediately adds urgency to the Bishop's demands.
    Anselm   He is the only one of the *nephews* to be named in the poem.

3   **Nephews**   a euphemism (indirect word) for 'sons'. The Bishop, as a Catholic cleric, has taken a vow of celibacy and therefore should not have children; however, in the same line he calls them by their proper title of *sons mine*.

4   Admitting they are his sons spurs him on to reminiscences about his former lover.

5   **Old Gandolf**   This is the first mention of the Bishop's rival churchman. *Old Gandolf* seems to have been his predecessor as Bishop.

6   **What's done is done**   This suggests acceptance of the past rivalry with Gandolf, and of his own past sin.

6–8   The repeated allusions to the death of his mistress not only serve to suggest pain and loss but also to act as a background to the Bishop's thoughts about his and all humankind's mortality.

9   The passing away of all that he has loved leads the Bishop to conclude it is obvious that *the world's a dream* – compare line 1.

10   **Life, how and what is it?**   The rather odd grammatical structure of the rhetorical question suggests that the Bishop is becoming less lucid. Nevertheless this phrasing has a sermon-like quality that reflects his position in life. The caesura after the question implies a puzzled pause before the Bishop once more focuses on his own situation.

11–12   **dying by degrees... dead night**   The repeated references to death, and the mention of night, create a gloomy motif in this section of the poem, reinforced by the alliteration that draws the reader's attention to the Bishop's approaching death.

13 **'Do I live, am I dead?'** Once again the rhetorical question draws attention to the confused state of the Bishop's mind, as he appears to struggle to understand his present state.

13–14 **Peace, peace… church for peace** This changes the mood of the poem as the Bishop seems to reflect on the tranquillity that the church offers. This is reinforced by the alliteration, which celebrates the calm of what he hopes will be his final resting place.

15 **I fought** Once again the mood of the poem alters.

16 **niche** a recess in the church where a tomb can be placed.

17 **cozened** tricked. Here Gandolf is seen as a cheat who has by illicit means gained a site for his tomb that the Bishop *fought* to save for his own.

18 Notice the use of alliteration again in this line. The words *Shrewd* and *snatch* characterize Gandolf's actions.

19 **carrion** rotting flesh of a dead animal. This description of Gandolf's dead body reveals the deep-seated contempt the Bishop feels for this man.

21 **epistle-side** the side of the church where the Epistle from the New Testament is read during Mass (the right-hand side as you face the altar). What do you make of the Bishop's description of the view from his *niche*? Why does it matter to him?

25 **basalt** dense, dark grey stone.

26 **tabernacle** canopy over a tomb.

28 **where Anselm stands** What is the effect of this phrase, occurring in the midst of the Bishop's description?

29–30 The freshness and delicacy implied in the *Peach-blossom* image of the marble's colour is balanced by the more earthy description of it as *the rare, the ripe/ As fresh-poured red wine*. The alliteration here helps to suggest that the colour is rich and satisfying. Do these two images reflect two different aspects of the Bishop's character, or simply two of nature's (or God's) gifts that he has loved?

31 **paltry onion-stone** cheap marble, which tends to flake (like an onion). This description of Gandolf's tomb creates an image of a peeling and flaking structure, one that is in his eyes contemptible.

32 **Put me where I may look at him!** His insistence that his own tomb should be placed within sight of Gandolf's suggests his desire to gloat eternally.

32–3 **True peach.../ the prize** The image of the *peach* is reiterated in these lines to describe the beauty of the marble of his tomb, but may also recall the beauty of his former mistress – perhaps she too was *Rosy and flawless*. The *prize* may refer to both her love and his prestigious tomb.

34 **Draw close** This phrase returns the reader to the beginning of the poem as the Bishop appeals directly to his sons. The caesura creates a pause that redirects the focus to an earlier event in the church's (and the Bishop's) history.
conflagration large, destructive fire.

35–6 The fragmented sentence structure here reflects the wandering of the Bishop's mind, at first concerned with the fire and the enigmatic reference to *much* that was saved balanced against *aught* (anything) that may have been missed. Is there a suggestion here that he did not behave honourably at the time of the fire? Does the imperative *Go dig* pick up an echo of the vague *aught* that may have gone missing from the church's treasures, and raise the question of where the *lapis lazuli* in the following lines came from?

41 **olive-frail** basket for gathering olives.

42 *lapis lazuli* semi-precious stone of an intense blue colour.

43–4 The similes that describe the stone are rich and sensuous. Although they both refer to biblical images, they create a picture of (respectively) violence and illicit desire, reinforced by the use of alliteration.

45–6 The description of what the Bishop has bequeathed to his sons seems appropriate to a worldly rather than a religious man – one who has not only enjoyed and valued the pleasures of life, but has acquired significant wealth.

46 **Frascati** town in a wine-growing area near Rome.

47–50 The imagined placing of the *blue lump* of *lapis lazuli* between the *knees* of the Bishop's statue on his tomb creates a startlingly physical image, while also serving to define him in terms of his desire for worldly treasures. Even in death he wishes to revel in the glory of owning this exceptional stone, and it is this image that directs his focus back to Gandolf as he imagines his rival bursting with envy. Here Browning brings together the Bishop's weaknesses by highlighting his childish desire for triumph over his enemy while still coveting worldly possessions even after death.

51 The image of the weaver's shuttle in this simile once again links the Bishop to the material world, although the image is taken from the Bible (see Job 7:6).

52–3 The rhetorical questions here refocus both the Bishop and the reader on the immediate problem: that of his imminent death and his desire for glory. The pause after the word *Black* creates the effect of a moment's thought as the Bishop continues to concern himself with the effect of the contrasting elements of his tomb.

56–63 **The bas-relief... Ye mark me not!** This rather long, rambling description of the sculpted bronze relief the Bishop wishes to have as a *frieze* on his tomb mixes pagan with Christian imagery, and sensuousness with the biblical morality of the Sermon on the Mount and the Ten Commandments.

57 **Pans and Nymphs** Pan is a Greek god of shepherds, flocks, and the countryside; he is associated with music, revelry and fertility. Nymphs are female spirits in the shape of young girls, frequently associated with Pan.
   wot know.

58 **tripod** three-legged stool, as used by the priestesses of Apollo.
   thyrsus ornamental spear or rod, often associated with Dionysus, Greek god of wine.

60 **glory** halo.

62 **Moses with the tables** According to Exodus 24:12, Moses received the Ten Commandments written by God on tablets (*tables*) of stone. Ironically, one of the commandments forbids the worship of pagan gods.

66 **beggar's mouldy travertine** a grave fit only for a beggar, made of mere limestone. Notice his derisive attitude towards beggars, even though Christian morality argues that the poor are close to God, as Jesus Christ was poor.

68 **jasper** a bright green stone that can be highly polished.

73–5 The images here of *Horses*, valuable *Greek manuscripts*, and *mistresses with great smooth marbly limbs* show that he intends to *pray* to *Saint Praxed* for worldly pleasures for his sons, rather than for their souls.

77 **Tully's every word** Marcus Tullius Cicero was a famous Roman orator (106–43 BCE), considered a model of Latin style.

79 **Ulpian** Gnaeus Domitius Ulpianus (170–228 CE) served in the Roman council. He was much less well known and his Latin was considered less pure and stylish than Cicero's (*Tully's*).

80–84 What do you make of this representation of the rites and ceremonies in the church, as the Bishop hopes to experience them from his tomb? Note that he refers to four different senses: *hear*, *see*, *feel*, *taste*. Are the church rites presented in a casual and even sacrilegious manner, or is his love for them genuine and moving?

82 **God made and eaten** The Bishop here makes a typically down-to-earth reference to the Catholic communion, in which the bread and wine offered to the faithful are thought to be transformed into the body and blood of Jesus Christ.

87 **crook** a long staff with a curved top, carried by Bishops as a symbol of office.

89 **mortcloth** the shroud that is used to cover the dead.

91–2 **yon tapers dwindle, and strange thoughts/ Grow** As the candles (*tapers*) burn low, so his life appears close to being extinguished, and his mind becomes confused.

93–8 In these lines Browning adopts a stream-of-consciousness style as the Bishop's thoughts dart from one idea to the next, blending different parts of his life together, and conflating *Saint Praxed* with Jesus's *sermon on the mount*.

97 **agate** a type of quartz stone, with a bright colour and fine grain.

98 **Latin pure, discreet** Is there a suggestion that this language is formal and conventional, so it can conceal indiscretions that other languages might reveal?

99 ELUCESCEBAT he was notable, or illustrious. The form of this word shows that *our friend* Gandolf has used a less pure form of Latin, whereas the Bishop is insistent that he shall have only the classical, purer form of the language.

102–3 The threat the Bishop now pronounces – to disinherit his sons – suggests his desperation to attain glory in death. It was common practice for wealthy men to leave their estates to the Pope in the hope that he would pray for them to be received safely into heaven. The Bishop's lack of certainty that he can trust his sons is illustrated by the pathos of the question *Will ye ever eat my heart?*, and his description of their eyes in lines 104–5.

106–11   The petulant tone of these lines and his insistence on even
greater glories for his tomb demonstrate his struggle against
his failing power.

108   **vizor**   mask.
Term   sculpted bust on top of a square pillar, used in classical art and architecture. The Bishop's love of art appears
to dominate his desires and serves to detach him from
Christian symbols, as once again he calls for pre-Christian
images.

111   **entablature**   stone slab.

115–17   Again the fragmented sentence structure demonstrates the
Bishop's anxious thoughts, yet also his powerlessness. Does
he show anger here?

116   **Gritstone**   coarse sandstone, often used as building material.

123   **leisure, leers**   The alliteration and assonance stress once
again the rivalry that drives the Bishop's thoughts as he
returns to his obsession with *Old Gandolf*.

125   **so fair she was!**   The final words of the poem, as he is left
alone to die, are not about his tomb, or his rival, or his
sons, but an exclamation about the beauty of his dead lover.
Thus Browning leaves the reader with an impression of the
Bishop as a man characterized by pride, envy, hypocrisy, and
worldliness, but also by a love of beauty.

The Laboratory

In this poem Browning explores the dire consequences of jealousy and hatred: the speaker is about to commit murder. Set in
eighteenth-century France (as indicated by the subtitle *Ancien
Régime*), this dramatic monologue invites the reader to watch
with the speaker as deadly poison is prepared for her to use on
the woman who is her rival in love.

During the Renaissance, poison was commonly chosen as a
murder weapon; it was easily obtainable from apothecaries (people who prepared medicines) and difficult to detect. It was
regarded as the obvious method of killing for a woman to use, as
it involved no violence, and physical strength was not necessary.
The reference in line 2 to *smokes curling whitely* perhaps suggests
that the poison being prepared here is arsenic.

Notes

1 **thy glass mask**   The use of the familiar second-person possessive pronoun *thy* suggests the speaker wishes to be on friendly terms with the apothecary, as she carefully fits the protective mask to her face to enable her to watch how he prepares the poison.

3 **devil's-smithy**   This compound noun is used to set the scene in the apothecary's laboratory. A *smithy* is a blacksmith's workplace, so the image conjured up is one of fire linked to Christian images of hell.

4 The quick repetition of the word *poison* here suggests the speaker's eagerness.

5 **they know that I know**   The repetition of *know* alludes to the issue of knowledge and power.

7 **they laugh, laugh**   The speaker's vision of the *He* and *her* of line 5 mocking her distress is reinforced by this repetition. She is suggesting that they gain pleasure from her suffering.

8 **I am here**   Standing alone at the end of the line, this phrase serves as a stark contrast to the *He*, *her* and *they* of the previous lines as the speaker asserts her control; she counterbalances what *they* think they know with the fact that she is not in the *Empty church* but in the laboratory. She is presented as having the real knowledge, in contrast to their ignorance.

9 **Grind, moisten, mash**   These onomatopoeic words suggest both the apothecary's energy and her relish at the activity she is watching.

10 **Pound at thy powder**   The alliterative phrase reinforces the intensity of the action and creates a sense of the speaker's pleasure as the poison begins to take form. She seems to savour the process of creating the poison, creating a malevolent and sinister atmosphere.

14–16 Notice that the adjectives and adverb in these lines are all incongruous in the circumstances, again reinforcing the pleasure she takes from watching her plans for revenge move forwards.

17–18 Rhyming *treasures* with *pleasures* underscores the speaker's perverted delight in the poisons. The image of the apothecary's products being *a wild crowd* suggests anarchy and rebellion, clearly linked to her intentions.

19–20 **an earring... a filigree basket**   The list of rich and delicate objects in these lines alerts the reader to the speaker's social status, touched on in line 12. These are all feminine adornments and paradoxically suggest innocent delight, whereas the speaker disturbingly links them to the power of *pure death*.

21–4 In this stanza the speaker fantasizes about the extent of her new-found power. The listing of *Elise*'s physical attributes demonstrates how disagreeable she finds the beauty of other women, and the final words *should drop dead* reinforce the malicious tone.

23 **pastile** a small stick or tablet that is burned to release a chemical (usually perfume).

25 **Quick – is it finished?** Note the speaker's mounting excitement. The caesura (pause) after this question allows us to imagine the apothecary showing the results of his labours. **The colour's too grim!** This petulant response suggests a childish desire to see the powder as something bright and beautiful – perhaps reflecting the way she imagines she will feel after committing the murder.

27–8 **turn, stir, try, taste** These verbs combine to slow the pace, and are suggestive of a long, lingering process before the moment of death, which the speaker intends to savour.

29 **What a drop!** The pace is quickened here as the speaker registers her incredulity at the small amount of poison that will be needed to despatch her rival.
no minion like me The contrast that is set up between the two women here hints at her belief that she is at a disadvantage, being small; *minion* also suggests subservience, as it is a word for a weak, dependent or low-status person.

30 **ensnared** This implies that the speaker believes the lover was trapped or lured away by the other woman. Is she trying to move all the blame from the man onto the woman?

33–6 There is a contrast here between the power the speaker believes her venomous hatred contains – she describes how she imagined just a stare from her *own eyes* would make her rival *fall/ Shrivelled* – and the real power that she now holds in her hand, the poison that *does it all*.

39 **Brand, burn up, bite** The alliterative trio of verbs reinforces the sense of her malice and sadism.

40 How would you characterize the mood of this line?

43 The force of her desire for her rival's death, and the power of a tiny quantity of poison, are brought together by the juxtaposition of the alliterative *delicate droplet* with *my whole fortune's fee*.

45 **gorge gold** The alliteration helps to create an image of the apothecary as greedy and amoral.

46 The speaker is clearly attuned to the apothecary's desires, and does she also invite the *kiss* as a sign of (self-)congratulation? This shocking invitation is made to sound casual, but even more unsavoury, by the parenthetical allusion to his age.

47 Her cool use of the imperative here focuses the reader on the fragile line between life and death, while the word *dust* echoes the Christian image of death: 'for dust thou art, and unto dust shalt thou return' (Genesis 3:19).

48 **next moment I dance at the King's** The final words of the poem remind the reader that the visit to the apothecary has been just an interlude in the speaker's busy social round at the highest levels of society. The reader is left to wonder at the lightness of tone the speaker adopts in contrast to the darkness of the deed just sealed.

Meeting at Night

Meeting at Night and *Parting at Morning* are frequently printed as a pair in poetry anthologies; they were originally published as one poem in two sections, before Browning divided them and gave them separate titles.

The poems are open to a number of interpretations; they contrast the mood of the speaker at night and in the morning, but the situation is not fully explained. Notice that there is no main verb in *Meeting at Night*; the poem's grammar suggests that the actions described are merely setting the scene for something more important or more fundamental.

1–2 The visual imagery here describes the sea, sky and landscape through the use of colours – *grey*, *black*, *yellow* – and creates a quiet and mysterious atmosphere.

3–4 Notice the energy in these lines, in contrast to the languorous mood of the first two, created by the words *startled*, *leap* and *fiery*. The sense of desire, energy and power perhaps characterizes the male quest.

5 **prow** the forward part of a boat. The image created is that of the boat *pushing* its way into the *cove* against the eddy of

the waves. This may also be read as having sexual overtones.

6   The onomatopoeic conclusion to this first stanza, with its *slushy sand*, creates a contrast between the urgency with which the boat has been steered into the *cove* and the sudden stillness, as the wet sand acts to *quench its speed*. Once again it is possible to interpret this line as having sexual overtones.

7   A contrast is created here with the first stanza, which has been characterized by the quest to reach the shore. The language becomes sensuous as Browning appeals to touch and smell to signal a change of mood as well as setting.

8–10   The pace is quickened and urgency is suggested by the rhythm, and through the use of monosyllabic (one-syllable) words, as the poem moves towards its climax.

11–12   The external sound of the *voice* is contrasted with the internal *beating* of the *two hearts*, suggesting an attachment that transcends language. How would you characterize the tone with which the poem ends?

Parting at Morning

Browning said that *Parting at Morning* is a 'confession of how fleeting is the belief' implied in *Meeting at Night* 'that such raptures are self-sufficient and enduring'.

1–2   The *sudden* sighting of *the sea* and the personification of *the sun* create a sense of the power and dominance of nature.

3   **him**   i.e. the sun. The sun is given a masculine persona; his *path of gold* suggests glory, riches and beauty.

4   The final line echoes the sentiments touched on in line 3 as the speaker places himself in the poem and suggests that, like the sun, his calling is to the *world of men* (i.e. wider society). Is the suggestion here that his work is the most important thing to him, rather than relationships? Or does the *world of men* suggest varied relationships and a place in society?

Love Among the Ruins

This poem is spoken by a shepherd in the Italian countryside, near a ruined city; his beloved is waiting for him among the ruins. It can be read as a kind of dramatic monologue, although it is not directed at a listener; the shepherd is alone and we hear his musings. The poem moves from a description of the landscape as it appears in the present to how it was in the past. It then moves to thoughts about the young man's lover, and fuses together the past and the present in the final stanza.

This poem has an unusual form and metre. Each stanza consists of six rhyming couplets, in which the first line has six feet (about 11 syllables) and the second line has one foot (three syllables). The long lines are formed mostly of trochees (a foot containing a stressed followed by an unstressed syllable). The short lines each contain a cretic (a foot of three syllables where the first and the last are stressed). This unusual metre creates a particular melody, like the rhythm of a song. It creates a meditative effect as the reader engages with the reflections of the shepherd. Ian Jack writes of this poem: 'The effect of the long lines, each followed by a short line... is curiously hypnotic, and the whole poem leads to the unanswerable affirmation in the final line' (*Browning's Major Poetry*, page 140 – see Further Reading).

1–2   The opening lines create an image of a pastoral scene and the rhyming *smiles,/ Miles and miles* suggests both the beauty of the evening and an expanse of undulating countryside.

5   The onomatopoeic *Tinkle* engages the reader with both the visual image and the sound of the sheep returning from the pastures. The assonance in *stray or stop* creates a visual image of the changing movements of the animals.

7   This line introduces the contrast between the quiet tranquillity of the present scene and the *city great and gay* of former times.

13   The caesura (pause) in this line re-focuses the reader on the present day. We are presented with a contrast between the horizontal plains of the present time and the vertical towers that characterized the city.

15   **verdure**   greenery.
      rills   small streams.

19   **domed and daring**   The alliterative phrase suggests both the symmetry of the *palace*'s architecture and the ambition of the occupants of the palace; describing the *palace* as *daring* creates

a metonym insofar as it characterizes the rulers within it.

19–21 Notice how the enjambment of these lines quickens the pace.

21 **hundred-gated** The compound adjective reinforces the idea of a tight enclosure.

25 Browning moves the reader's attention back to the present and contrasts this with the lost glories of the past.

31 The image here engages the reader with the passions and vicissitudes of life, as pain and pleasure are balanced one against the other.

33–4 The balancing of opposites is repeated here as the men are seen lusting for *glory*. The word *lust* suggests a desire linked in some way to the *shame* they dread, and *tame* suggests submission and compliance.

37 **turret** small tower.

39 **caper** shrub that grows in Mediterranean regions.
gourd the fruit of a plant related to pumpkin, squash and cucumber.

41 **houseleek** plant with fleshy leaves and pink or red flowers.

45 **burning ring** This image emphasizes the intensity of the chariot race.

47 **minions** servants, followers.

49 This line returns the reader to the present and echoes the first stanza.

53–4 **in undistinguished grey/ Melt away** The movement of time is signalled by this allusion to the fading light.

55 **a girl with eager eyes** Here the poet introduces the ultimate object of the shepherd's reverie. The alliterative description of the girl's eyes suggests her liveliness and her desire for the young man.

59 **breathless** The idea of the girl's impatience and fervour is developed here.

65 **causeys** causeways (raised roads).

71–2 The idea of the urgency, desire and passion of the lovers is reinforced in these lines through the verbs *rush* and *extinguish*, emphasizing the quick movement of the couple. Their passion obliterates the visual and the verbal.

73–8 Notice the images Browning uses to create a sense of the power, glory but also corruption of the former city.

79 **burns** The image of burning maintains the contrast between the fiery heart of the lost city and the tranquil greenery that now characterizes the landscape.

80–81 This terse summary of human recklessness and corrupt
behaviour is created through the triadic structure *folly, noise
and sin*. It contrasts dramatically with the silent and joyful
world of love and desire that the embrace of the lovers created at the end of the previous stanza.

82 This phrase recalls the *hundred-gated circuit of a wall/
Bounding all* in lines 21–2.

84 The assertion in the poem's final line has been anticipated
in the title of the poem, and in its clarity and simplicity it
seems to celebrate love as a pure emotion that easily transcends all the complications of corruption, the desire for
power, and human vanities.

Up at a Villa – Down in the City

In this poem Browning evokes the immediacy of day-to-day
life in Italy at the time when he and Elizabeth Barrett lived
there. However, Browning subverts the stock satiric theme of the
limitations of country life in contrast to the excitement of the
city. Life in the country was commonly characterized as an
isolated, unrefined and even ignorant existence, for example in
seventeenth- and eighteenth-century plays where country gentle-
men are invariably presented as buffoons who are behind the
times and easily duped when they come to town. Although
Browning enjoyed some aspects of the Italian city scene himself,
the speaker of the poem (described as *an Italian Person of Quality*)
is ultimately presented as an object of satire. The unusual form
of this poem (beginning with triplets – three-line stanzas rhyming
aaa – and moving through stanzas of increasing length) serves to
create a sense of a torrent of chatter, and reinforces the impression of the speaker as rather foolish.

1–3 The first triplet focuses the reader on an important issue of
the poem, the need for plenty of *money* in order to enjoy
the delights of city life. The repetition of *such a life* suggests
an active participation in the excitement of the daily round.
However, the speaker in fact sees his role more as that of an

observer *at the window*, ironically living his life vicariously through the activity of other people.

4 **by Bacchus** The use of this common Italian oath (Bacchus was the Roman god of wine and intoxication) develops the image of the speaker as pleasure-loving and self-indulgent.

6 **no more than a beast** The image of life in the country being no better than that of a *beast* reinforces the idea that country life is characterized by lack of refinement and stupidity.

7–10 The speaker creates an image of isolation here, but ironically his description of the position of the villa offers the reader a sense of the wild beauty of the countryside.

10 **turned wool** i.e. become like a sheep's.

11–13 A contrast is created with the unspoilt wildness of the countryside as the houses in the *square* are described as *stone-faced*, and all in *four straight lines*. The images here suggest containment, limitation and order, and the compound adjective *stone-faced*, together with the simile *white as a curd*, suggests there is a coldness and lifelessness to the view that the speaker celebrates.

17–20 Once again the speaker offers a contrast to the bustle and activity of the city with images of a protracted winter and the dull *brown ploughed land*, as opposed to the gaudy colours of the town, the *Green blinds*, bright sunlight and *fanciful signs* of the preceding stanza.

21–5 The rhetorical question that opens this stanza sets the tone as the speaker contemptuously dismisses the glories and beauties of nature, concluding with an image of the tulip as a *bubble of blood*. This unpleasant simile concisely conveys the speaker's attitude to the natural beauty that surrounds him.

26–30 The language here is characterized by active verbs that bring to life the energy and constant movement of city life. The alliterative description of the sculpted horses in the fountain, which seem to beat the water with their hooves, re-inforces the idea of the vitality of the city as these animals, created by an artist, have a vigour that is lacking in the flesh-and-blood *oxen* in the country, which *steam and wheeze* (19).

27 **foam-bows** rainbows in the foam or bubbles.

28 **pash** smash, trample.

31–7 Images of death characterize this stanza, as the speaker continues to reject life in the country. Ironically, however, his descriptions also offer the reader an impression of unspoilt beauty in which nature is full of splendours to anyone with a sympathetic eye or ear. The bustle of the city is here replaced by the simple beauty of the *fireflies* that weave themselves among the *hemp*. The image of the *stalks... a-tingle* creates a sense of subtle movement as the stems seem to quiver and vibrate with the movement of the insects.

34 **thrid** thread.

38–42 Contrast the sounds used here to characterize the animation of the city with those described in the previous stanza. There is a real sense of the speaker's pleasure as he rejoices in the variety of the city scene, and the reader is presented with a series of tableaux in which something is happening all the time.

39 **diligence** horse-drawn coach for passengers and mail.

42 **Pulcinello-trumpet** trumpet call summoning people to watch a puppet show, an early version of Punch and Judy.

44 **three liberal thieves were shot** The dismissive tone the speaker uses when alluding to the execution of those he terms *liberal thieves* (as if it were just another of the city's entertainments) suggests his indifference to the movement for political reform and Italy's liberation from Austria, a cause that had Browning's full sympathy.

45–6 These lines allude to the election of Pope Pius IX in 1846, who at first encouraged the liberals. However, after the rebellion against Austria was crushed in 1849 he became reactionary. Grand Duke Leopold II of Tuscany, who had also given hope to the liberals, was forced to leave Florence in 1848. He returned in 1849, supported by Austrian troops, and his *little new laws* were pro-Pope and anti-liberal; for example he repealed the Tuscan constitution in 1852. Browning's allusions to these political events serve to distance the speaker of the poem from the poet and maintain the satiric presentation of his character.

47 **marge** margin.
    Don title given to an Italian priest or man of high status.

48 The dismissive tone adopted towards these great men of literature again reinforces the impression of a speaker who lacks taste and judgement.

49 **the skirts of Saint Paul has reached** has achieved almost as much as St Paul.

50 **unctuous** excessively pious or earnest.

51 **our Lady borne smiling and smart** An image of the Virgin Mary is often carried in religious *processions*. Here, there is a suggestion of vulgarity in the way she is presented.

52 **seven swords** symbols for the seven sorrows of the Virgin Mary.

53 The sounds of the city are presented through onomatopoeic language, but interestingly the instruments that produce this cacophony are the *drum* and the *fife*, both usually associated with a call to arms.

55–7 In the closing stanza the speaker returns to his opening subject, that of money, or rather the lack of it. His tone is one of resignation: *And so, the villa for me, not the city!* The commercialism of city life is seen in the references to *wine, at double the rate* and *a new tax upon salt*, but the speaker remains undeterred in his preference for such a life. The reader is left with an image of a character who is shallow and rather foolish, but has he nevertheless painted a convincing picture of the pleasures of the city?

A Woman's Last Word

Unusually for Browning, in this poem we hear the voice of a woman. It is characterized by a simple lyrical eloquence and is concerned with reconciliation, a desire to be forgiven and, it seems, to be ruled by her lover. The title ironically refers to a saying popularized by D.W. Jerrold in *Mrs Caudle's Curtain Lectures* (1845) that a woman always has the last word in an argument.

The poem's short lines and elliptical syntax suggest perhaps that the woman is struggling to speak through tears, and in this sense it can be argued that Browning offers a sympathetic portrait. The lyrical form and the fragmented line structure appear to mirror the emotional turmoil of the speaker. Alternatively, however, as the speaker begins by suggesting that the man goes to sleep rather than argues, and ends with wishing to fall asleep herself, we might read the poem as the voice of a woman attempting to persuade a man to give up thought and analysis and to turn away from truth. It is useful to consider both of these readings when studying the poem. What is your own response to Browning's imaginative interest in a woman's experience of love?

1–4   The first stanza is characterized by a soft and plaintive tone as the woman appears to desire reconciliation.

8   **Hawk on bough!**   This image refers to the idea of their love being in danger of destruction, as the predatory *Hawk* lurks near the vulnerable *birds* on the branch. The image is also linked to the *tree* of knowledge in line 16. Is the implication that knowledge is dangerous? See the headnote and Note to lines 15–16.

15–16   This borrows a phrase from Shakespeare: 'How sharper than a serpent's tooth it is/ To have a thankless child!' (*King Lear*, Act I Scene IV). The *serpent* is also the form the Devil takes to tempt Eve in the Garden of *Eden* (19) to eat the *apple* (17) from the *tree* of knowledge, as told in the Bible (Genesis 3), and in Milton's *Paradise Lost*.

17–20   The biblical imagery appears to be used by the woman to negate the man as he is instructed to turn away from the tree of knowledge; reason and understanding can be seen as the death knell of passion and desire, and can result in the loss of *Eden*. However, this concern about loss does not directly include the man she addresses – she makes it clear that the *we* who may *lose our Edens* are *Eve and I*.

21–4   There is a tone of self-abasement in these lines as the woman calls for tenderness and security. However, it is possible that her request for him to *Be a man and fold me/ With thine arm* carries a hidden reproach that he has not in the past assumed this role.

25–8   If we follow the argument that this woman's apparent desire to be reconciled is in fact a way of attaining power, these lines can seem like those of sirens who flatter and lure men to their destruction. Alternatively, it is possible that there is an element of male fantasy here as the speaker begs to subsume her identity in that of the man. Is the poet suggesting that this is appropriate behaviour for women?

29–32   The image of the offering up of both *flesh and spirit* reinforces the idea of a complete loss of identity.

33   **That shall be to-morrow**   These words seek to delay the surrender described in the previous stanza, suggesting

perhaps that she intends to maintain a sense of self-determination and that her words belie her real intentions.

37–40 The concluding stanza can be read as a clear affirmation of love, or alternatively as a statement that she has attained her object, that of being loved and desired, and to have her lover forget the quarrel that has led to her monologue.

Fra Lippo Lippi

This is another of Browning's dramatic monologues, and like much of his writing it springs from his interest in Italy, its art and artists. Filippo Lippi was a painter who lived between about 1406 and 1469 and worked in Florence. (For a painting by Lippi, see the illustration on page 153.) For the details of the painter's life and personality, Browning used Vasari's *Lives of the Most Excellent Painters, Sculptors and Architects* (see page 91).

Lippi was orphaned at an early age and became a monk ('Fra' means 'Brother'). In the monastery, it is said, his love for drawing was more important to him than all the monks' attempts to give him a formal education, and he received the training that enabled him to become a successful artist.

The poem opens in the early hours of the morning in Florence's red-light district, and the reader is presented with a monk who has just been apprehended by the night watchmen. It seems that after having spent three weeks confined indoors by his patron Cosimo de Medici (see the illustration on page 195) in order to create paintings of saints, he has been lured by the sound of merriment outside. He has escaped from his room with the intention of joining in with the revels. What follows embraces the themes of passion, poverty, religion, art-making and the nature of beauty.

1–2 Note the vivid and engaging opening. The scene is set in the street and it involves at least two other people besides Fra Lippo Lippi, as he refers to *torches* being held close to his face. *Brother* implies that the speaker is a monk and *by your leave* is a formal expression. However, *clap* is a lively and colloquial term.

3 **Zooks** an exclamation that comes from 'Gadzooks', which probably means 'God's hooks', the nails that pinned Jesus to the cross. It is a mild expletive, reinforcing the idea of Lippi's determination and lack of restraint.

6 **sportive ladies** i.e. prostitutes.

7 **Carmine** the church of the Carmelite order of monks, to which Lippi belongs.

8 **harry out** drive or search out.
zeal (excessive) eagerness.

10 **softling** soft, harmless creature. The suggestion is that these (represented by the *wee white mouse*) are feminine, in contrast to the masculine *rat*.

17 Why do you think Lippi hesitates before revealing the name of his patron, the famous Cosimo de Medici (1389–1464, an important Florentine politician and patron of the arts)?

20 **gullet's-gripe** grip on the throat. The language once again suggests Lippi's liveliness, and his use of black humour in referring to hanging.

21–4 Lippi launches into an attack against the leader of the watchmen, suggesting that his reputation will be tainted by the officious behaviour of his men.

23 **pilchards** The metaphor of small fish implies the watchmen have little respect for ordinary citizens.

25 **to a tittle** 'to a T', precisely.

26 **Why sir, you make amends** How does the tone change here, and what do you think this reveals about the character of Lippi?

31–9 **I'd like his face... you style me so** In these lines Browning celebrates the eye of the painter; Lippi now begins to see his captors as models for his paintings.

34 **John Baptist** John, who baptized Jesus, was killed by being beheaded on the orders of King Herod. Two famous paintings by Lippi, 'John the Baptist Bids Farewell to his Family' and 'The Feast of Herod', are alluded to.

37–8 He is so excited by what he sees that he asks for *chalk* or *wood-coal* so that he can sketch it.

40 **brother Lippo** He affirms his identity.

41 **take** please.

45   Lippi begins to tell what led up to his being found in the
       streets *past midnight* (4).

46   **carnival**   the time for entertainment, feasting and pleasure
       before the onset of Lent, when fasting and restraint are
       called for.

47   **mew**   cage or prison.

48–9   **saints and saints/ And saints again**   The repetition suggests
       his boredom with the subjects of his paintings.

50   **Ouf!**   This mild exclamation reinforces his disgust at being
       locked away from pleasure and enjoyment.

60–61 **zooks, sir flesh and blood,/ That's all I'm made of!**   What
       does this comment, and the words of the songs he quotes
       in lines 53–7 and 68–9, reveal about his nature?

62   The alliteration and listing here emphasize the speed and
       manner of his escape.

67   **Hard by St Laurence**   next to the church of St Laurence
       (San Lorenzo, in which Lippi painted an Annunciation scene).

73   **Jerome**   Saint Jerome, who died in 420; a man noted for his
       asceticism (rejection of worldly pleasures) and often depict-
       ed by Renaissance painters striking himself on the chest
       with a rock *to subdue the flesh*. He is clearly a figure who con-
       trasts with Lippi's love of pleasure.

81–92 Consider how the tone of the monologue changes here.
       Why do you think this is, and what effect does it have on
       the presentation of Lippi?

88   **Aunt Lapaccia**   After the death of his parents, Lippi was
       brought up by his aunt, who soon placed him in a monastery.

89   He poignantly but comically refers to his aunt's hand as *a sting-
       er*, implying that she has many times punished him with blows.

92–7   The dialogue between the *fat father* and the young Lippi is pre-
       sented with a characteristically comic tone, but it also highlights
       the hypocrisy of the religious order as the boy is encouraged to
       renounce the world (98) in return for being fed and housed.

98–101 The absurd list of what the impoverished boy is supposedly
       renouncing culminates with the explosive word *Trash* to
       characterize all that belongs to the unimaginably rich *poor
       devils of Medici*.

103–5 Note the earthiness of Lippi's motivation for becoming a
       monk.

109–11 His failure to learn any Latin except *amo*, meaning 'I love',
       serves to reinforce the idea of the sensuality of his nature,

and it is fittingly woven into a snatch of the song he has
heard on this carnival night.

121   **the Eight**   Florence had eight magistrates.

126   **admonition**   reprimand, warning.

130–33   **Scrawled, Joined, Found, And made**   Notice how the verbs
beginning each of these lines suggest both his ceaseless
activity and the variety and liveliness of his drawings.

130   **antiphonary**   service book containing the responses to be
spoken in church.

135   **The monks looked black**   As well as their anger, does the
word *black* suggest the monks' lack of vision?

136–41   The direct speech here communicates the Prior's excitement
at the possibility of being on a par with another order of
monks, the *Camaldolese*, in having someone with artistic
talent who can *do our church up fine*.

142   **daub away**   These words suggest that the Prior sees Lippi
more as a painter and decorator than an artist, and again
reinforces the lack of imagination of the monks.

143–4   Notice Lippi's characteristically straightforward and lively
response to this opportunity.

145–162   This immensely long sentence once again adopts the listing
technique to reinforce the sense of urgency and variety. The
images tumble out, signposted by prepositions: *First, then,
From, To.* They become more and more detailed, and culmi-
nate in the description of the murderer and the people who
react to him. What is striking about this description?

145   **the black and white**   black-robed monks (Dominicans) and
white-robed monks (Carmelites).

148   **cribs**   petty thefts.

168–71   **'That's the very man!... it's the life!'**   The spontaneous
enthusiasm of the *simple* monks is expressed in words that
emphasize how lifelike and lively the paintings are. Contrast
this response with that of *The Prior and the learned* (174).

178   **devil's-game**   What do you think they mean by this?

184–7   Notice Browning's use of ellipses, dashes, contradiction,
parenthesis, repetition and tautology in these lines. What is
the effect of these techniques?

189   **Giotto**   Giotto di Bondone, about 1267–1337, also of
Florence, is often considered the first of the great painters
of the Italian Renaissance.

196   **Herodias**   mother of Salome, and wife of King Herod; she

asked for the head of John the Baptist. Our attention is drawn
to hypocrisy of the Prior here, as he admires the drawing of
the *white smallish female with the breasts* and associates it
with his *niece*. (Do we suspect her real relationship to him is
somewhat different? See also lines 209 and 387.) But he
quickly corrects himself and links the image to the biblical
story of Herodias.

198 **Now, is this sense, I ask?** This question introduces the
argument that the representation of beauty does not prevent a painter from putting *soul* into his work.

221–69 In these lines Lippi reflects on how his life has turned out,
and explains his attitudes.

227 See lines 17–18.

231–40 Lippi feels undervalued by his seemingly learned critics. The
vivid colloquial phrase *Fag on at flesh* (237) describes his
efforts through their eyes – continuing to labour at depicting
the real bodies of individual human beings, rather than
concentrating on spiritual or religious messages. The phrase
reflects both his resignation at this criticism and his
contempt for such views.

235 **Brother Angelico** Giovanni da Fiesole (about 1395–1455),
better known as Fra Angelico, one of the most highly
regarded painters of the early Italian Renaissance.

236 **Brother Lorenzo** Lorenzo Monaco (about 1370–1425), who
may have taught Fra Angelico.

241 **they're the likeliest to know** Does he mean this, in humble
acceptance of his lack of learning, or is he being ironic?

242 **They with their Latin?** Compare lines 109–11.

250–54 **my whole soul revolves... In pure rage!** What reasons does
Lippi offer for being found out in the streets this evening?
How does Browning develop his character at this point in
the poem?

250 **the cup runs over** See Psalms 23:5.

254–9 **The old mill-horse... May they or mayn't they?** Lippi
reflects on the hypocrisy of humankind through the
metaphor of the horse and grass.

262 **You don't like** i.e. you pretend not to like.

263 **You do like** i.e. you pretend to like.

266–7 **I always see... A-making man's wife** According to Genesis
2, God made Eve as a wife for Adam in the Garden of
Eden. Lippi's directness helps him find links between the

physical and the spiritual. What do you make of his *lesson learned* about *The value and significance of flesh* (268)?

270–315 In this section Lippi launches into a tirade to support his attitude to painting and to life, and reinforces it by indicating that he has a talented pupil who *picks my practice up* (278). Once again Browning through the voice of Lippi puts forward the argument that the artist should reflect *The beauty and the wonder and the power* (283) of the world.

276 **Guidi** Tomasso Guidi, the influential Florentine painter known as Masaccio (1401–28). He is in fact more likely to have been Lippi's teacher (or at least a great influence on him) than his pupil.

277 **Hulking Tom** a translation of the nickname 'Masaccio' (see above).

307 **cullion** rogue, rascal.
hanging face face of someone who deserves to be hanged.

316–22 This dialogue between the Prior and Lippi is related, of course, from Lippi's viewpoint. Consider how Lippi presents his ideas on religion and how these contrast with those of the Prior.

318 **matins** morning prayers.

323 **Saint Laurence** This saint was martyred by being roasted to death on a gridiron (see line 328 – he is *the Deacon*).

324 **Prato** site of the cathedral where Lippi painted frescoes.

327 **phiz** slang term for 'face'.

336–40 Lippi directly addresses the watch, attempts to excuse himself again and asks for their indulgence. Notice the colloquial tone.

337 **God wot** God knows.

343–6 He offers to *make amends* by creating a painting for St Ambrogio's church, which the watchmen will be able to go and see. What kind of painting does Lippo suggest he will create (347–59)?

347 **cast o' my office** example of my work.

351 **orris-root** the root of the iris flower, used in perfume.

357 **Job** central character in the Bible's Book of Job.

358 **Uz** Job's homeland.

375 **camel-hair** *Saint John* the Baptist (374) wore clothing made of camel-hair.

377 *Iste perfecit opus* Latin: 'this man made the work'. These words appear beside a figure in one of Lippi's paintings.

378–87   Lippi refers to his skill at hovering in the background and escaping from difficult situations, especially ones that involve amorous adventures.

380   **kirtles**   skirts.

381   **hot cockles**   a children's game, but here a euphemism for a sexual liaison.

392   **There's the grey beginning**   The poem concludes with a return to the present circumstances and Lippi's concern to avoid being seen outside as the dawn begins. What do you make of the choice of *Zooks!* as the last word in the poem?

'Childe Roland to the Dark Tower Came'

The title of this poem comes from the end of Act III Scene IV of Shakespeare's *King Lear*. Edgar, on the run from those who want to kill him, is pretending to be a madman, and during a raging storm on a wild heath he speaks these lines:

Childe Rowland to the dark tower came,
His word was still: Fie, foh, and fum,
I smell the blood of a British man.

Browning is said to have been inspired to write the poem by these lines, and by a picture of a gloomy scene he had seen in Paris, by the figure of a red horse on a tapestry in his own drawing room, and by a square tower he had seen in the Carrara mountains of Italy. When asked about this poem 30 years later, he said that it had no allegorical meaning but was simply a work of fantasy. He claimed that it came upon him as a kind of dream and that 'I did not know then what I meant... and I'm sure I don't know now. But I am very fond of it.'

On one level it can be read as a poem that celebrates heroism, and remaining loyal to an avowed purpose when all hope is lost. Alternatively, it can be seen in the context of stories about quests, popular in medieval literature and in the tales of King

Notes

Arthur and his knights. 'Childe' was a title for a young man who had not yet become a knight.

1 **My first thought was** Immediately we are drawn into the poem by the voice of the narrator, who addresses us as if in mid-situation. He tells us what is going on in his mind but gives us no background information. This is a technique Browning uses in other dramatic monologues, such as *Fra Lippo Lippi* and *Andrea del Sarto*.
he lied This plunges the reader into a worrying world of uncertainty.

2 **hoary** old and grey.
malicious spiteful, malevolent.

3 **Askance** with a sideways glance; suspicious or disapproving.

4–6 **and mouth scarce able... Its edge** This is an image of a man who can hardly hold back his delight at the *working of his lie*, so he purses his lips to suppress the smile of *glee* that threatens to appear, as if it had a will of its own.

6 **one more victim** This suggests a history of such meetings and deceptions.

7 **staff** stick.

8 **ensnare** entrap.

9 **posted** positioned.

10 **skull-like laugh** This alliterative simile introduces the idea of death; it suggests a mocking tone.

11–12 **'gin write my epitaph** begin to write the record of my death. This compounds the horror, as he imagines this final inscription will not be on a tombstone but grotesquely scratched with a *crutch... in the dusty thoroughfare.*

13 **If** Beginning with the conditional suggests that the speaker is giving thought to his actions, but by line 15 it is clear he has decided to follow the proffered directions.

15 **Yet acquiescingly** This implies that he has given in, and has left the wiser choice of path in favour of one beset with danger. This marks the beginning of his quest to find the *Dark Tower*.

16–18 The lack of *pride*, as well as *hope*, indicated in these lines creates a joyless mood for the quest, and the speaker's only consolation is that *some end might be.*

17 **descried**   caught sight of.

19 The alliteration in this line creates a sense of the endless-
ness of the quest, compounded by the word *wandering*,
which suggests a lack of purpose and direction.

20–22 Juxtaposing the complete lack of hope with the image of
the possible *joy* being *obstreperous* (unruly and difficult to
control) serves to create an even bleaker mood.

23–4 In these concluding lines of the stanza, Browning hints at a
paradox as he creates an image of the heart fluttering with
excitement – *the spring/My heart made* – when it finds that
some kind of closure, even though it is likely to be *failure*,
is finally in prospect.

25–30 This stanza develops the mood of desolation, using the
extended image of the sick man who realizes his end is in
sight and feels calm and at ease, knowing that it is soon to
be *all... o'er*.

31–6 There is a certain irony in the description here of the man
approaching death, as he listens to the preparations for his
funeral. He does not wish to disappoint his friends so his
only desire now is that *He may not shame such tender love* by
continuing to live.

37 **quest**   This is an important word in the poem. The narrator
goes on to contextualize it.

39 **'The Band'**   Defined in the following line, this is a name
for all those who, like himself, have tried to find the Tower
but have failed to do so.
to wit   that is.

41–2 **that just to fail... should I be fit?**   These lines seem to offer
some reason for the speaker's quest, as he identifies himself
with all the knights who have attempted it before him. He
seems to seek a place with them in the annals of history
even if it is because, like them, he has failed. The final
rhetorical question alerts the reader to the narrator's doubts
about himself.

43 **quiet as despair**   The mood is set by this simile, as the
speaker sets off on the path indicated.

45–8 **All the day... catch its estray**   The pathetic fallacy here –
where the weather seems to reflect human moods – develops
the idea that the quest is hopeless, as even the setting sun
appears to mock him with a *Red leer* as the open, empty
wasteland catches hold of the stray wanderer.

50 **Pledged to the plain** He has made a commitment in his choice of path; notice the suggestion that his honour is now involved.

56 **starved ignoble nature** Nature is personified; *starved* implies lack of growth.
throve grew or prospered.

57 **as well expect a cedar grove!** The narrator makes a grim joke about the wasteland.

58–9 His despairing mood is reflected in the landscape. *Cockle* is a weedy plant, and *spurge* is a bush that has a bitter juice.

60 The idea of a *burr* (a prickly seed-carrier) being a *treasure-trove* develops the grim humour through the use of hyperbole.

61 Nature personified is linked with the negative and disquieting triplet *penury* (poverty), *inertness and grimace.*

62–6 When Nature speaks, it is *peevishly*; her words suggest supreme indifference and a trust only in the fires of the *Last Judgment* to bring about any change in the landscape.

64 **It nothing skills** it makes no difference.

66 **Calcine its clods** literally, turn the hard *clods* of the earth to a powder by the impact of high temperatures – here, the fire is the one that is prophesied in the Bible for the *Last Judgment*, a purifying blaze that will allow the earth once again to flourish.

68 **bents** stalks of coarse grass.

70 **swarth** dark.

70–71 **bruised as to baulk/ All hope of greenness** This suggests that any sign of life is immediately destroyed or prevented in this wilderness.

71–2 **'tis a brute... their life out** It is as if some *brute* stalks the land, crushing all life.

73–5 The simile of the grass being like a leper's hair creates an image of disease and putrefaction. The conceit continues with the image of mud being *pricked* as if by *blades* of grass and yielding *blood.*

76–8 The description of the horse creates a ghastly image by linking *stiff, a-stare, Stood stupefied, service* and *stud* in an alliterative list that culminates in the idea that the horse belongs to *the devil.*

79–81 The use of colour imagery in *red* and *rusty* implies a bloodiness about the horse, and its state of being *Alive?... dead* serves to reinforce the fact that it is a horrific distortion of nature.

80 **colloped** This is an obscure word perhaps meaning 'sliced' or 'ridged'.

84 How does the idea of pain caused by wickedness link back to the *cripple* we met at the beginning of the poem?

85–90 The mood lifts for a moment here as the speaker imagines taking a glass of wine, and conjuring images of *earlier, happier sights*.

91–102 The positive mood is denied as the memories of the narrator seem to reflect the landscape. The positive image of the knight Cuthbert, with his *curly gold* hair, is replaced by *disgrace*, and *cold* replaces the *new fire*. Likewise the image of Giles, *the soul of honour*, turns from a pleasant memory to one of horror as he is pictured with a *parchment* detailing his treason pinned to his chest.

103–4 The focus returns to the present and the ghastly nature of the narrator's *darkening path* – note that the adjective suggests that worse is to come.

106 **howlet** owl.

109–10 The image of the *sudden little river* appears almost like a magical manifestation. However, the link to the *serpent* suggests that the river's winding nature conjures up images of the devil (who took the form of a serpent in the Garden of Eden, according to Genesis 2).

112–13 **a bath/ For the fiend's glowing hoof** The image of the devil is reinforced here.

113–14 **the wrath... spumes** the personification of the river as showing *wrath* makes it terrifying. It is described as spitting out its anger.

114 **bespate** bespattered.
flakes and spumes foam.

115 **So petty yet so spiteful!** Once again negative human characteristics are attributed to the river.

116–20 Here mood and landscape merge in a pathetic fallacy of submission to *despair*, *suicidal* thoughts and *wrong*.

121–6 The language here develops the image of the nightmare world as the narrator crosses the terrifying river. Consider the effect of the accumulated details of *dead man's cheek, spear... thrust, hollows, tangled... hair, beard, water-rat* and *baby's shriek*.

128 **presage** feeling or intuition about the future. Hope and despair are captured in this line, as optimism is immediately replaced by profound disappointment.

133 **fell**   deadly.

cirque   circular space, arena.

135 **mews**   confined place.

141 **brake**   toothed wheel; also an obsolete name for a rack (instrument of torture).

143 **Tophet**   place of horror associated with human sacrifice, described in the Bible's Old Testament.

147 **Desperate and done with**   This alliterative phrase reinforces the image of a barren and hostile wasteland.

148 **mars**   spoils, ruins.

149 **rood**   quarter of an acre.

151–6 Consider how the metaphors of disease and the use of onomatopoeia in this stanza convey ideas of distortion and decay.

157 The mood of desperation is reinforced by the heavy rhythm of this line.

160–2 The image of the *great black bird* does little to raise hopes that it could be a useful *guide* or offer any sense of hope, so the reader is left to question why the mood is lightened when the narrator reflects that *perchance* it may be so.

160 **Apollyon**   the destroyer, a name given to the ruler of hell (also the name of a monster in John Bunyan's *Pilgrim's Progress*).

161 **penned**   feathered.

167 **solve it, you!**   The abrupt appearance of this direct address to the reader seems to hint that the speaker has lost faith in his own judgement and challenges those who read his story to solve the mystery.

169–71 **trick... mischief... bad dream**   These words all serve to propel both the reader and the narrator in another direction, towards more confusion and away from any possibility of resolution.

171–2 **Here ended, then,/ Progress this way**   The finality of this assertion suggests the narrator's belief that his quest is at an end, and the following caesura (pause) lends weight to his conviction.

179 **nonce**   moment.

180 The exclamation that concludes this stanza conjures up the state of shock he experiences when realizing that *This was the place*.

182–4 **The round squat... In the whole world**   The description of the long-sought Tower may make it sound dull and disappointing, but it is nevertheless unique.

184–5   **The tempest's mocking... the timbers start**   The image of
the *shipman* mocked by the storm, who strikes his boat against
the unseen shelf of rock, acts as an allegory for the position the
narrator now finds himself in with the Tower before him.

190–92   What is the effect of the personification of the hills here?
The words *hunting*, *game at bay*, *stab* and *creature* all serve to
create a picture of a hunted animal about to meet its death.

192   **heft**   hilt.

194–202   **Names in my ears... I knew them all**   Browning creates a
kind of tableau here, as the narrator focuses not on his own
plight but on those who went before him.

198   **knelled**   rang slowly and solemnly, or tolled, like a funeral
bell.

203–4   The final two lines create a kind of epiphany (an intense
moment of understanding or perception) as the narrator
blows his horn, and Browning returns the reader to the
poem's title. It is not success or failure that is important,
but the fact that Childe Roland is *Dauntless*; he has not faltered, and has pursued the quest to its end.

Love in a Life

This poem forms a pair with *Life in a Love*, and in each of these
poems the lover is pursuing his mistress. Browning wrote in a
letter to Elizabeth Barrett: 'In this House of Life, where I go, you
go – where I ascend you run before, – where I descend, it is after
you.' It is possible to view the house and rooms in this poem not
just literally but also allegorically as the 'house of life' that the
two lovers share. If read in this way the *suites*, *closets* and *alcoves*
of the final two lines would represent the woman's thoughts or
emotions.

1–2   The image of a search or quest is foregrounded in this
opening line, and reinforced by the use of the verb *hunt*.

3   The assertion that both the speaker and his mistress inhabit
the same space allows for the allegorical reading that they
are of one mind and share the same thoughts and ideas.

4–5   The fragmented structure of these lines reflects the speaker's need for reassurance as he addresses his own *heart*. The pause before the change to a more positive tone in *Next time* creates a sense of the speaker catching his breath before insisting that it will be *herself* he finds. What do you make of the word *trouble*, used to describe the after-effects of her presence?

6–8 The concluding lines of the first stanza appeal to the senses of touch, sight and smell as life appears to be breathed into inanimate objects by the mere hint of the beloved's presence. These images are suggestive of both her vitality and her beauty.

9–10 The tone becomes less optimistic at the beginning of the second stanza.

12–13 This rhyming couplet emphasizes the central image of the poem.

15–16 **such suites... to importune!** The poem ends on a positive note, with the speaker not only undefeated but seemingly eager to take advantage of the varied opportunities he has to engage with her. How do these lines add to the sense of the unlimited fascination she holds for him?

Life in a Love

This poem forms a pair with *Love in a Life*, above, which begins with a seemingly hopeless quest but ends with the suggestion that in some way the lover is destined to succeed. In this poem, however, the reverse is true – despite the assertive opening, by the end of the poem the lover appears sure to fail. Is this in fact the same lover, having finally grasped the fact that a true union with his mistress will always elude him?

1–3 What sense of the speaker's mental state do these extremely short lines create? Is he desperate, over-confident, troubled, obsessive?

6 The alliterative balancing of *loving* with *loth* (unwilling, reluctant) illustrates the distance between them and sums up the emotions of the poem.

7 Browning uses the traditional idea of courtly love here, where the 'knight' is on a quest for the love of the beautiful lady who spurns his advances.

8 **fault**   This can be read simply as 'failure', but it is also a
hunting term, used to describe the situation when the
pursuing hounds lose the scent of their prey. This image
gives the poem a darker tone (see Interpretations page 163).

9–10   The rhyming couplet seems to offer a sense of resolution,
as the speaker presents himself as resigned to his *fate*.

11   The rhetorical question changes the tone of the poem again,
as the speaker seems to become more determined to
maintain the pursuit.

12–15   Just as in '*Childe Roland to the Dark Tower Came*' (page 51),
it seems that it is the quest itself that is of most importance, rather than the success of the pursuit.

17   **deep**, **dust**, **dark**   The alliteration suggests the gloomy, bleak
mindscape of the speaker.

18–20   The mood changes here as once again the reader is carried
along with the rise and fall of the speaker's emotions; with
the loss of *old hope* comes the growth of *a new one*.

20–22   The poem concludes as it began, with very short lines. The
speaker seems to define himself in terms of his quest. Does
he take a perverse kind of pleasure in the fact that it will
last for *Ever*, as he can hope for no resolution? His *Beloved*
(line 3) will always remain *Removed* – notice the pattern of
echoes and rhymes between these lines and lines 1–3.

The Last Ride Together

In this poem Browning explores the experience of failure in love.
In many ways it can be read as a valediction (a farewell or leave-
taking), in the same vein as John Donne's poem *A Valediction
Forbidding Mourning*. Throughout the poem, the lover is presented as striving to find value in his experience, and trying to
transcend failure by turning it into some kind of success. The last
meeting of the lovers is presented as an image of eternity, as if
time can be frozen and he can continue to enjoy the moment
forever.

Interestingly, this poem has been parodied by several writers,
the best one being *The Last Ride Together (From Her Point of View)*
by James Kenneth Stephen (1891). You may like to look for this
on the Internet.

1–5   The use of anaphora (repetition) with the word *since* in these lines creates the impression of building up a philosophical argument.

6–7   The tone appears at first to be celebratory.

8–9   The caesura (pause) in line 8 changes the mood as the speaker asserts that pleasure is to be found only in *memory*.

12–13   The alliteration in these lines creates a visual picture of the mood and *pride* of the woman.

15   **breathing-while**   The compound noun slows the pace and creates a space for tension to develop.

17   To balance the *breathing* referred to in line 15, here the circulation of his *blood* seems to restart after a pause; such is the relief he feels when she grants his wish for a *last ride*.

21   **deified**   made into a god. This implies that his relationship with his lover is sacred and raises him above the mere human.

22   This line signals one of the important ideas of the poem, that of living in the moment and trying to halt the passage of time.

23   **if**   This word introduces a simile that is completed in lines 32 and 33, with the repeated *Thus*. Notice that all the natural images in the stanza are linked together, and all are associated with *heaven* (line 31).

24   The alliterative compound adjectives create a sense of abundance, and the language becomes increasingly sensuous.

31   The idea of a spiritual love transcending life and death is alluded to here, as *flesh* is replaced by *heaven*.

34–6   **My soul... in the wind**   What do you make of this image of the *soul* as a *scroll*? Once again, the speaker defines his experience in spiritual terms.

38   **awry**   gone wrong.

45–6   These lines introduce another important idea in the poem – the nature of success and failure, and whether the former is even possible in human lives.

47–9   **it seemed... on either side**   The idea of a life beyond the earth-bound is reiterated here, as the ride stimulates the speaker's imagination.

56–9   The use of anaphora and rhetorical questioning engages the reader with the emotions of the speaker, who attempts to justify his failure by pointing to the impossibility of perfect success for human beings.

59   **the fleshly screen**   the limitations or barriers imposed by the body.

60 This line refocuses the speaker and the reader on the immediacy of the moment, and the sensual aspect of love and desire.

66 This recalls the last line of *Love Among the Ruins* (page 32), and it can be seen to have sexual overtones; the energy, movement and pleasure of the ride create a sensual and even erotic atmosphere. It also alludes to the idea, developed later in the poem, that expectation is better than the attainment of desire, as lines 61–5 alert the reader to the temporary and fragile nature of the success and glory that can be gained by the ambitious.

67–77 The focus of the speaker in this stanza turns to art, and in particular poetry. Browning explores the limitations of his art, suggesting – as he does in several other works – that art or poetry exist simply as one form of creative endeavour to draw out life's meaning. The tone is at times mocking and scornful as the speaker sets his own passion against that of the artist.

68 **Your brains beat into rhythm** This alludes to the discipline and even regimentation required to produce poetry.

77 In contrast, the speaker celebrates the glory of passion and love, symbolized by the ride. The imperative *Sing* commands the poet to celebrate the rhythms and creative act embodied in the ride.

78–88 In this stanza the speaker turns to other arts, as he addresses a *sculptor* and a *man of music*.

80 **Venus** goddess of love; a popular subject for classical sculpture.
whence from which.

81 **fords the burn** crosses the stream.

82 The balance between *You acquiesce* and the rhetorical question *shall I repine* (be miserable) brings together the acceptance by the *sculptor* that the beauty of his *Venus* cannot compete against a living *girl*, with the speaker's acceptance that he cannot succeed in love.

87 The speaker suggests that however great its achievements, music – like other arts – is subject to changing fashions.

88 Once again Browning employs a contrast within the line, as the work of the artists – like the speaker's efforts in love – have taken away their *youth*, but the speaker still has the ride, a fact emphasized by the use of the present tense (*we ride*).
in fine in short.

89–93   The speaker continues his philosophical enquiry as he reflects on what would have happened if *fate* had decided to offer him *bliss* through success in love.

90   **sublimate**   purify, elevate.

91   **bond**   contract or agreement (with *fate*).

92–6   The speaker attempts to imagine how he could pursue or desire heavenly *bliss* if he had *bliss here* (line 90) on earth through love.

93   **dim-descried**   dimly perceived.

94–5   The alliterative *goal* and *glory-garland* evoke the feelings of happiness and satisfaction he imagines experiencing if he had achieved success in love.

97–8   The speaker admits defeat in his philosophical *quest* here, as he sets up a dichotomy (division into two parts) between the earthly pleasures of love and the bliss to be anticipated in heaven.

99   This statement returns the reader to the idea that the expectation of delight is better than any pleasure achieved; both kinds of bliss, that connected to love and that to be hoped for in *heaven*, still remain *beyond this ride*.

100   The speaker returns his focus to the woman. The caesura in this line signals the expression of a new thought.

101   **What if**   These words introduce the idea, developed in the rest of the stanza, that perhaps he has attained heaven after all – if this moment is destined to last for ever.

101–3   **fair and strong… first discerned**   These adjectives and phrases describe the speaker and his mistress (the *We* of line 104) at this moment in time. They are in the prime of their lives, and *life's flower* seems almost within their grasp; so is this experience, this anticipation of bliss, heaven itself?

104   **fixed**   This word returns us to the question of art; the two lovers might attain the unchanging quality of a work of art.

106   The paradox here echoes the ideas of the Romantic poet John Keats in *Ode on a Grecian Urn*, where he describes lovers represented in art:

> Bold lover, never, never canst thou kiss,
> Though winning near the goal – yet, do not grieve;
> She cannot fade, though thou hast not thy bliss,
> For ever wilt thou love, and she be fair!

Art reflects a moment of life frozen in time, so that the lover it depicts is always in a state of anticipation; it is a world in which experiences can be *old yet new*. Keats's poem, like Browning's, acknowledges the situation of failing to realize one's desires, but turns it into a celebration of the fact that failure and disappointment, too, are indefinitely postponed.

108   This image re-affirms the idea of the moment being fixed for *eternity*.

109   **prove**   be shown to be.

110   The repetition of the present-tense verb *ride* emphasizes the sense of a continuing present, and draws together the movement, energy and anticipation that the speaker now celebrates as the culmination of all his desires.

The Patriot

In this poem Browning depicts the fickleness of public opinion. The speaker describes how he was once greeted by the people as a hero, but now, a year later, he is to be executed as a traitor. As the poem is not given a particular time or place, and does not offer explanations for either the hero-worship or the condemnation, it seems to offer a universal message about the vagaries of politics and the shallowness of popular opinion. The subtitle, 'An Old Story', reinforces the message that this is a familiar aspect of human nature.

1–2   The repetition of *roses* emphasizes the power of this emblem of love and beauty. This image is reinforced by the choice of *myrtle*, a plant sacred to Venus, the goddess of love, and also seen as a symbol of love.

3–4   The language here creates a sense of the extraordinary enthusiasm at the speaker's arrival in the city, created through the use of the imagery of *house-roofs* and *church-spires*. The former seem to *heave and sway*, presumably with the crowds of people, while the latter are said to have *flamed* with flags. There may be proleptic irony (foreshadowing future events) in the choice of these verbs, as they

can suggest danger and destruction; the speaker's reminiscences are coloured by the events described later in the
poem.

6–7 Browning continues to build up a kaleidoscope of visual
and aural images in these lines. The synaesthesia (blending
of the senses) in line 6 and the movement in line 7 serve to
reinforce the sense of celebration and the fervour of the
crowd.

8–10 The use of direct speech in these lines – even though it is
not reported speech, and the narrator is merely speculating
– strengthens the sense of connection he feels he had with
the people, and reinforces his belief that he would have
been able to command them to do anything.

10 **They had** they would have.

11 **Alack** archaic word for 'Alas' (an expression of regret).
The use of archaic language seems to place the poem in a
distant past, although the issues it raises remain very
current. The tone of the poem changes at this point.
leaped at the sun The speaker outlines the extent of the
sacrifices he has made for the people through this metaphor.
The implication is that he was extremely ambitious on their
behalf and has performed amazing feats.

13 The balanced structure of this line reinforces the idea of his
dedication and commitment to his country.

16–17 The break between these two lines slows the pace of the
poem and directs the reader to the image of the watchers at
the *windows*, who are only those who are confined to their
homes by sickness (*palsied*).

19 **Shambles' Gate** The name suggests that this was originally
the site of slaughterhouses and butcher's shops. The tension
is developed again through the use of the caesura (pause)
following these words.

20 **trow** archaic word for 'believe'.

21 **in the rain** The use of the pathetic fallacy (where the
weather seems to reflect human emotions) creates an
atmosphere of darkness, sorrow and suffering.

25 **my year's misdeeds** What tone can you detect in this
phrase? Do you think there is irony, resignation, regret,
anger, contempt?

26 This balanced line not only expresses the speaker's

acceptance of his fate but also highlights the cyclical nature
of life; the speaker's literal entrance and exit of the city
have been described, and now he is to *go* from the world.

27 **triumphs**   public processions to celebrate victories (as in
ancient Rome).

dropped down dead   notice the blunt, alliterative description
of what is also to be the speaker's fate at the *scaffold* (line 20).

28–30 The concluding lines reinforce one of the key messages of
the poem: the fickleness of humanity. Pathos is created as
the speaker accepts his fate, but he optimistically looks
forward to being rewarded – and being *safer* – in heaven,
where *God shall repay*.

Andrea del Sarto

This poem complements *Pictor Ignotus* (page 17) and *Fra Lippo
Lippi* (page 39) in that it also describes an Italian Renaissance
painter from Florence, and offers some insight into Browning's
views on art. The contrast between Lippi and Andrea is that
Lippi believes in himself and his work despite its public reception, whereas Andrea is a painter who has gained much public
acclaim but believes that his work is little more than technically
competent. Compare, also, the attitude of the speaker in *Pictor
Ignotus* towards praise and blame. (For a portrait by Andrea, see
the illustration on page 176.)

Like Fra Lippo Lippi, Andrea del Sarto (1486–1531) is
described in Giorgio Vasari's *Lives of the Most Excellent Painters,
Sculptors and Architects* (1568). Andrea del Sarto, referred to as
'The Faultless Painter', was invited to become the court painter
for the French king, Francis I. After a year in his service, Andrea
asked permission to return home to Florence to see his wife
Lucrezia, the other character in this poem. The king agreed, and
gave Andrea a sum of money to purchase Italian artworks for the
French palace while he was away. According to Vasari, however,
Andrea was so besotted with his wife that he allowed her to persuade him to spend the money on their own home in Florence
instead, which caused a scandal and meant he could never return
to France. This situation forms the setting for the poem.

1 **But**   As with many of Browning's monologues, the poem begins mid-scene, signalled by the use of the connective. A *quarrel* has taken place before the monologue begins.

2 **my Lucrezia**   These words both identify her as his wife and also suggest possessiveness.
for once   This makes it clear that quarrelling is not uncommon between these two.

3 **all shall happen as you wish**   The reader is alerted to Andrea's desire to keep his wife happy – at what cost?

6, 7 **own**   The repetition of this word suggests Andrea's complete capitulation as he agrees to the terms and conditions of her *friend's friend*.

8 The payment for this work is to be given to his wife. This again reinforces his devotion and desire to sacrifice himself in return for his wife's affection.

9 **Will it? tenderly?**   The repeated questioning implies he is need of reassurance that his wife will respond to him *tenderly*.

11–19 How does Andrea present himself in these lines? Consider the word *wearier*.

15 **Fiesole**   village on a hill above Florence.

21–2 The focus here is on the sensuous pleasure of holding his wife's hand; we see the imaginative and sensuous engagement of a true artist. Her hand is a synecdoche for *a woman of itself*.

26 **serpentining beauty**   Does this phrase suggest her character, as well as her physical presence?

29–30 The repetition of the possessive pronoun *my* reminds us of the opening of the poem. We are offered a glimpse of his inner turmoil as he refers to her as *everybody's moon* on whom *everybody looks* and *calls* her *his*. It is suggested that Lucrezia has more than one admirer, but interestingly Andrea recognizes in line 32 that she is *no-one's*. Is Browning presenting Lucrezia as a self-possessed, modern woman?

33 **You smile?**   How does this question change the tone of the monologue?

35 **common greyness**   This implies dullness, and lack of worth.

36 **twilight**   This seems to symbolize the state of his career, their relationship, and even his life; all seem to be past their best in his own eyes.

38 **(That's gone you know)**   The pathos of his feeling that she

no longer has pride in him is emphasized by the use of
parentheses, and the phrase *you know*.

39 The effect of the listing is to emphasize that his lack of belief
in himself covers all areas of his life. The phrase *toned down*
reminds the reader that he is an artist who sees his life in terms
of colour tones or shades, and in this case they are fading.

44–5 As in lines 35–6, there is a sense of endings and of loss.

49 **twilight-piece** painting depicting a scene in twilight.
Love The direct address to Lucrezia gives the impression
of Andrea thinking aloud.

51 **fettered** chained.

53 **turn your head** What effect is created by this phrase?

57 **cartoon** preparatory sketch. It is a simple drawing, yet even
in this, he acknowledges, he is supremely skilful.

63 **Do easily** Does he see this ease as a blessing or a curse?

65–6 **the Legate's talk... in France** Andrea acknowledges that
his work is well received both at home by the *Legate* (the
Pope's representative) and abroad in the French court.

74–5 **you smeared/ Carelessly** Lucrezia is seen here as careless of
his work.

79–96 How does Andrea present himself in contrast to those who
have an apparently lesser skill? Consider what he means in
lines 83–4.

93 **Morello** a mountain near Florence.

94 **hue** colour.

105 **The Urbinate** the person from Urbino (a reference to the
painter Raphael, 1483–1520, see lines 119, 131, 136, etc.).

106 **George Vasari** See headnote.

112–14 **A fault... He means right** Andrea raises the question often
explored by Browning about the relationship between accurate representation within a painting and the power of all
the meanings communicated by a work of art. Andrea
makes the reader and Lucrezia aware that he clearly understands the difference.

117 **Out of me** out of my power.

118–19 Now the poem takes a new turn as Andrea moves from cas-
tigating himself to refocusing on Lucrezia who, he suggests,
has not been the 'muse' or inspiration that he has needed.

120–32 How does Browning present Andrea's ideas about the way
he feels Lucrezia has let him down? Consider the way he
describes her beauty, in contrast to her *mind* (126).

Notes

130 **Agnolo** Michelangelo (1475–1564), the great Renaissance
painter, sculptor and architect.

132–3 **I might have done it for you... Perhaps not** The uncertainty and doubt reflect the state of the speaker's mind.

136 Andrea now turns the argument away from Lucrezia and
back onto himself as he acknowledges, through this rhetorical question, that these great artists were not dependent on
a woman for their inspiration.

140 **And thus we half-men struggle** Once again pathos is created as Andrea says that he (like most human beings) has only
half the resources he needs to accomplish great things. The
suggestion in lines 137–9 is that most have either the *will* or
the *power*, but not both.

142–3 He implies that he is glad not to be given too high a reputation
in this world, so that God will still reward him in the next.

146 He fears an encounter with noblemen from France – see
headnote.

149–65 How does the speaker present his time at the French court, and
in what ways does he feel he attained some status and glory?

149 **Francis** the French king.

150 **Fontainebleau** the French royal palace.

166 **And had you not grown restless** Once again we hear a note
of regret in the speaker's voice, but he dismisses it.

169 **I'm the weak-eyed bat** Why do you think Andrea characterizes himself in this way?

170 **grange** barn, granary.

175 Like the artist he is, he desires to *frame* her *face* in his hands
as in a picture.

176 Once again the use of the possessive pronoun attempts to
contain the woman he feels he has sacrificed his reputation for.

177–9 Andrea draws a contrast between the way his works will be
received and discussed and those of Raphael, and he con-
soles himself that people will know that in his art the
model for the *Virgin was his wife*. Literally this refers to the
Virgin Mary, but metaphorically Andrea attempts to see his
wife as innocent and pure and only possessed by himself.

178 **The Roman** i.e. Raphael.

183–93 Here Andrea repeats an anecdote to Lucrezia in which he
suggests that Michelangelo had told Raphael that he (Andrea)
could be as great an artist if he had the patronage of (was
pricked on by) the same *popes and kings* (192).

194 **indeed the arm is wrong**   Andrea backs up his anecdote by
pointing out a flawed detail in Raphael's painting.

197 **Ay, but the soul!**   What is Andrea's conclusion about
whether it is better to paint faultlessly, or with inspiration?

199–200 It seems that he has lost his wife's attention, as he is forced
to tell her again whom he is speaking about.

203–4 The allusions to his wife's smile change the tone and mood
of the poem, but there is also pathos, as if she smiles for
him only rarely.

205–6 Andrea's dependence on Lucrezia is reaffirmed in these
lines as he asserts that he could work better if she were to
sit with him each evening.

207 Are these the only terms in which Lucrezia can *comprehend*
(206) and value his work?

208–10 The onset of *dusk* is created in the poem through attention
to the landscape, light and sound.

209 **Morello**   See Note to line 93.

211–14 **Come from the window… may forgive me**   How would you
describe the tone here? There is a sad contrast in that *the
melancholy little house* on which he spent the king's money
had been intended to make the couple *so gay*. In characteristic self-condemnatory style, Andrea asserts that *God is just*,
but this is juxtaposed with the rather pathetic hope for the
king's forgiveness.

214–18 **oft at nights… cement them with**   Here Andrea presents
his guilt through visual images, as he says in his imagination
he sees bricks joined not by *mortar* but gold, *fierce* and *bright*
as if it has the power to wound him.

218 **his**   i.e. King Francis's.

219 The juxtaposition of the two sentences in this line clearly
highlights Lucrezia's carelessness for her husband's feelings,
and his sad obsession with gaining her love.

220 The *Cousin*'s visits seem to be frequent and, as with the
euphemism *friend* in line 5, it is suggested that this is in fact
one of his wife's lovers.

221–2 **loans, gaming debts**   These words suggest Lucrezia's extravagance and financial mismanagement, for which her husband must pay with his art.

226 **pay my fancy**   Does the suggestion of a sordid financial deal
here suggest that Lucrezia is the one who is prostituting herself, or that Andrea is the one who is degrading himself?

226–33   **Only let me sit... its worth**   Once again the tone is set by the colour imagery the painter chooses. All is *grey* and he yearns to be back in France or to have Michelangelo praise his work again, within the hearing of his wife.

238   **demurs**   objects, protests.

241   **scudi**   silver coins.
     ruff   fashionable collar or neckband, usually frilled or pleated and made of fine fabric.

242   **Love, does that please you?**   Consider how Browning has built up to the pathos of this question, and uses this and the following line to focus on the compromises the painter has sunk to.

244   Once again the speaker adopts a thoughtful and reflective style, but the words *old age* strike a new, personal note – compare lines 35–6 and 44–5.

245   This line encapsulates the speaker's acceptance of his fate through its balanced structure. He *regrets little* on the one hand, and would *change still less* on the other.

246–56   Here he offers a concrete example of that balance as he sees the wrong to the French king balanced by the fact that his *father and... mother died of want* (250) and that although he has worked hard, he has *not been paid profusely* (255).

257–9   The most important *balance* that Andrea seeks is in his relationship with his wife. Here he seems to renounce any claims on more of her love than she has been prepared to give him.

260–61   He considers the possibility that God might offer him chances to create better art in heaven.

262   **Meted**   measured out.
     reed   measuring rod.

263   **Leonard**   Leonardo da Vinci (1452–1519).

264–6   **the three first... I choose**   He is forced to acknowledge that the three great painters he mentions are wifeless, and for him there's still Lucrezia. In these final lines, he asserts his choice – *I choose*. The use of the present tense and simple monosyllables confirms that this, simply, is how it is.

267   Andrea urges the woman he loves to comply with her lover's demands and to *Go*. The *whistle* is in itself a sign of disrespect, but Andrea colludes with his wife's infidelity as he knows it is the only way to keep her. In the end he knows he has chosen her rather than fame, reputation, or even his art.

'De Gustibus —'

The title is taken from the Latin proverb, 'De gustibus non est disputandum', meaning, 'there's no disputing about tastes'. This poem takes the form of a lyric in which Browning extols his love of Italy, *the land of lands* and his adopted country. The poem contrasts an English country lane with the mountains and coast of Italy.

In the first part of the poem Browning addresses a friend who loves the English countryside, and he imagines that after death the friend's *ghost* will wander among the beauties of *an English lane*. He then goes on to describe the type of country he himself loves *best in all the world*.

2   The parenthetical statement acknowledges that he is assuming, for the purposes of the poem, that the feelings or the effects of love can survive death.

4   The compound noun and compound adjective in this line offer a sense of movement but also of the fragility of natural beauty.

4–5   The use of a feminine rhyme (in which the final syllable is unstressed) produces the effect of soft echoes.

5   **in the hazel coppice**   This image invokes a feeling of security as the trees are solid, dependable features of the landscape. A *coppice* is a dense group of small trees or shrubs that are maintained by regular pruning, so the scene is one of human interaction with nature rather than wildness.

6   **if the good fates please**   This parenthetical phrase suggests that the harmony implied in the surrounding lines is conditional, and depends on chance.

9–13   The perfect rhymes in these lines create an echo that is pleasing to the ear and so reinforces the delight of this pastoral scene.

14   This second stanza opens with a contrast in tone – the first person *I* is used, and the statement is affirmative.

15   **precipice-encurled**   The compound adjective is suggestive of both danger and romance.

16   The word *gash* is alliteratively linked to the compound adjective *wind-grieved*, and both create a feeling of discomfort and damage. The *Apennine* is the mountain range that runs the length of the Italian peninsula. An untamed

wildness is suggested here, as Browning pictures the elemental forces that dominate the landscape.

17 **fellow**   friend, colleague. Browning here directly addresses the *you* of the poem again.

18–20   In this parenthesis, which parallels the one in line 2, Browning imagines the possibility of loosening the *bands* that will tie his *spirit* in death, so that it can *come again to the land of lands* (Italy). The repetition and rhymes here create a celebratory tone in which Browning fuses the image of his freedom after death with the wild freedom of the landscape.

22   **cicala**   large, winged insect that makes a high-pitched droning sound.
drouth   drought. The alliteration here, together with the image of the insect, serves to emphasize the power of the sun and the harshness of the landscape.

24–5   **red-rusted, iron-spiked, fruit-o'ercrusted**   The series of compound adjectives describe the one remaining tree that acts as a *sentinel* (guard). Its uncompromising structure is emphasized, and its age and durability are foregrounded by the colour imagery.

28–9   **the great opaque... without a break**   Note the alliteration and assonance in the description of the sea, highlighting its dominance and its vast size.

30–32   In contrast to the enduring quality of nature, the house – with art painted (*frescoed*) on its walls – *for ever crumbles*, and its decay is highlighted by the use of the words *fragment* and *blisters*. Once again Browning highlights the transitory nature of human existence and even of human art, in contrast to the durability and power of nature.

33–8   Here the description of the house and landscape are enlivened by a brief, colourful anecdote of a girl bringing a generous supply of *green-flesh melons* and at the same time delivering news that the *Bourbon* king has been shot and wounded. Notice the comic effects of the rhyming of *king*, *wing* and *sling*, and of *melons* with *felons* (criminals); the light-hearted, almost flippant tone of the description matches the anarchic response of the girl, who shows sympathy for the would-be assassins rather than the monarch.

39   Notice the use of the possessive pronoun here. What tones can you detect in this line, summing up as it does all the descriptions above?

40 **Queen Mary's saying**   During the reign of Mary I (1553–8), England lost control of Calais, its last possession in France. According to Raphael Holinshed's *Chronicles of England, Scotland and Ireland* (1577), Mary said that after death, should her body be opened up, the word 'Calais' would be found written on her heart.

45 **she**   i.e. Italy. Browning asserts that he and Italy are lovers and will be so forever. What do you make of the contrasts between the Italy described in this stanza and the England of the first stanza, which seems by comparison quiet and tame? You might also contrast the depiction of his love of Italy with the image of the lovers in the English lane, who will *pass... too soon* (line 10).

Women and Roses

Browning wrote this poem in a single day at the beginning of 1852. Having worked hard on an essay about Shelley, he determined to write a poem a day from New Year's Day. *Women and Roses* was one of the first of these, which he said was inspired by a magnificent basket of flowers sent to his wife as a present. The poem is a *dream* (1) about three roses that are encircled by women: the first group are women of the past, the next are living at the present, and the last are yet to be born.

1–3   The poem opens with a rhetorical question, one that suggests there will be some judgement of the women the speaker is about to describe. By framing this discussion of women within the context of a *dream*, Browning distances his responses from reality.

4–7   The repetition of *round* here suggests the encircling of the roses by the women, but it also presents a picture of continual movement, reinforced by the simile *like a dance of snow/ In a dazzling drift*. This is a strange paradox when we learn that these women have in fact been *faded for ages* and are contained by the poet and sculptor who have created (or re-created) them.

8–9   In these lines there is a sense of energy, immediacy and passion associated with the vitality of life, created through the alliterative phrase *Living and loving and loved to-day*.

10–11 **Last, in the rear... yet unborn** The last group of the
women are *maidens... yet unborn* who, it seems, appear in all
their *multitude*.

11 **to one cadence** This image suggests that within the confines of the speaker's imagination all these women move
with the same rhythm.

12 **my rose tree** What do you feel is the significance of the
use of the possessive pronoun *my* at this point?

13–15 This second three-line stanza or triplet returns the reader to
the image of the rose tree itself, and the speaker now apos-
trophizes one of its flowers: *Dear rose*. However, what is
introduced here is the image of death, and the rhyme
scheme alerts us to this rose's imminent demise and decay.

15 **unimpeached** unhindered. The bee that fertilizes the flowers passes by the dead bloom without being attracted to it.

16–18 These lines suggest the male desire to have women submit
to him and to stay the same, so that he can *fix*, *fire* and
freeze them like works of art. The alliteration here reinforces the idea of containment and the imagery is taken from
artistic techniques: an artist preserves subjects either on
canvas, in stone or in clay.

19 The rhetorical question here presupposes the women's
ability to make their admirer suffer, and their desire to
make him abase himself, literally and metaphorically *at
their feet*.

20–24 The idea of possession, already touched upon, is reasserted
here as love is presented in terms of ownership. These
women, however, are already beyond such possibility, having the *pallid* skin of the dead. They seem to tantalize the
speaker with ideas of *poesy* (poetry) and *passion* but it is all
in vain as they are unattainable, being mere spectres that
circle one of the roses on the tree of his imagination.

25–7 In this next triplet the tone changes to one of celebration as
the speaker glories in the beauty of living women. This rose
is described as having a vibrant colour (*ruby-rimmed*) and
being full of the sweetness of life (*nectar-brimmed*). The
image of the *cup* of the flower overflowing with *nectar* creates an unambiguously sexual symbol.

28–32 The sensual language and the use of the image of the *bee
sucked in* create a sense of desire and passion.

33 The image of the *cincture* (literally a belt or sash) suggests

the idea of encircling, developed through the extended metaphor of *Girdle me* (35), and also alludes to love-making in
the suggestion of clothing being loosened.

34   There is a sense here of being lost in physical passion; this
replaces any spiritual yearning of the *soul*.

35–6   **But no... my rose tree**   The speaker concludes that he is
to be disappointed, as the moment is fleeting and transitory.
The *old measure* (dance) is resumed and the women continue
to circle their rose on his spectral rose tree.

37–9   The final triplet turns our attention to the rose *without a
thorn*, representing women who are as yet *unborn*, so seem to
offer all the potential but none of the threat of love. The
rhymes add to the sense that these women encapsulate all
the promise of love, beauty and passion but pose no risk to
the speaker.

40   The call for *wings* echoes John Keats's poem *Ode to a
Nightingale*, in which he refers to 'the viewless wings of
poesy'. The speaker seems to be calling for a flight into the
realms of imagination and the abstract, in which he might
be able to connect with the very essence of womankind.

43   **Sprung from the dust**   The biblical reference (see Note to
The Laboratory line 47) reinforces the idea of the cyclical
nature of life.

46–8   The speaker's insistence that in his art he can create the
perfect woman and shape her *to his mind* returns the reader
to earlier images of containment in the poem. However,
the poem concludes on a pessimistic note as, like the dead
and the living women, the women yet to be born also
encircle their rose on the speaker's imagined tree and thus,
although they offer the idea of perfect love – one that has
no thorns – they are unattainable and defy the speaker's
attempts to fix them in his art.

Two in the Campagna

Browning wrote this poem during his time in Italy, when he lived
there with his wife Elizabeth Barrett. Interestingly, although it is
a sensual and passionate poem, it concerns itself with the limitations of human love. Setting the poem in the *campagna* – the
countryside that surrounds Rome – Browning exploits the pastoral

tradition in which the countryside is often presented as a wild place where the rules of society do not apply (as in Shakespeare's *As You Like It*). Throughout the poem, Browning plays with the concept of ideal love, but the *campagna*, or wild space, offers only a transient escape from the limitations of human nature and society, and in consequence the speaker is left saddened.

3–4   The association with nature in these lines sets the scene of the poem and introduces the reader to the idea of nature acting as a catalyst to the freedom of the imagination.

5   The allusion to morning and to *May* suggests new beginnings, as spring is traditionally associated with young love.

6   **I touched a thought**   The use of synaesthesia (the blending of the senses) in this line creates an image of the mystery of love and the limitations of language in expressing ideas about it.

7   **tantalized**   The idea of the elusiveness of thought and the difficulty of distilling it into *rhymes* (9) is reinforced here. What do you feel is the effect of the simile in lines 8–9?

11   **Help me to hold it!**   The imperative tone indicates the speaker's desperation in trying to fix a fleeting impression within the bounds of his thought processes. There may be a suggestion that he believes his lover can act as a 'muse' or inspiration to enable him to give voice to his emotions through the medium of poetry.

12–20   The speaker here seems enchanted by the wild beauty of the landscape, and the description suggests that he is almost able to trace his abstract thought through the different elements of the countryside scenes he is observing. The image of *yellowing fennel, run to seed* suggests a profusion of fertile life that echoes his thoughts, and the *Five beetles* that are *blind and green* and *grope/ Among the honeymeal* can be seen to symbolize the speaker's struggle to give voice to various fleeting thoughts and feelings. The assertion *I traced it* and the insistence of the imperative *Hold it fast!* paradoxically confirm the transitory nature of thought and love.

15   **weft**   thread.

21   **champaign**   flat, open countryside.

23 The balancing of *Silence* and *peace* with *joy* and *passion* seems to suggest that the gentle beauty of the countryside offers an inner calm and harmony where desire is satisfied and the mind is quiet and still.

26–9 The repetition of *Such* focuses the reader on the abundant glories open to humanity away from the constraints and pressures of the city.

31 **How say you?** The direct question changes the focus of the poem and the speaker goes on to question the possibility of ever having complete control of our emotions.

36, 41 **I would** The speaker now clearly expresses his wish that human experience could be perfected.

39 **Where does the fault lie?** This suggests that the problem cannot be resolved.

40 **wound** This image reinforces the idea that love brings pain. According to popular myth, Cupid's arrow opens up a wound for which there is no remedy, and over which people can have no control.

41–5 In these lines the speaker expresses his desire to be as one with his lover, and the image in the words *set my heart/ Beating by yours* creates the idea of two synchronized hearts moving through time together as one unified being. This is developed through the image of him drinking his fill at her *soul's springs*, again reinforcing the sense of a spiritual union.

48 **Catch your soul's warmth** These lines suggest a capturing of that moment when lovers meet and there seems to be a spiritual communion between them.

50 The final line of this stanza refocuses the mood of the poem as one of sadness, because the moment of perfect communion is found to be as transitory as ever.

51–5 The speaker now presents himself as like a feather for each wind that blows. He seems to have no self-determination but is blown *like the thistle-ball* in any direction.

57 **Where is the thread now?** This question takes the reader back to the opening of the poem and the tantalizing threads that lead nowhere.

58–60 The exclamation *The old trick!* reflects his experience of repeated disappointment. While he continues to feel the possibility of *Infinite passion*, he knows that it is unattainable and that *finite hearts* can only *yearn* for true fulfilment.

Prospice

Unlike in most of Browning's work, in this poem we hear the voice of the poet himself. It is a voice that embraces the challenge of death, and expresses the wish to approach *The post of the foe* without fear and in full consciousness. Browning wrote *Prospice* shortly after the death of his wife.

There are similarities between this poem and *'Childe Roland to the Dark Tower Came'* (page 51), as Childe Roland also completes his journey and at the end of the poem he is more than ready to meet his foe, in whatever form it takes.

Title *Prospice* is Latin for 'Look ahead'.

1 **Fear death?** The poem opens with a challenge, created through the use of the rhetorical question.

1–4 **the fog... nearing the place** A mysterious and cold world is created through the images of *fog*, *mist*, *snows* and the *blasts* of strong winds, suggesting a haze that offers no clear sense of place. The landscape and the weather seem hostile and also to indicate that the traveller's journey is soon to be at an end.

5 The *night* appears to take on a force of its own and Browning continues to use the pathetic fallacy (where weather conditions reflect human emotions).

6 The personification of death as a personal *foe* stresses the private and lonely aspect of dying; it perhaps suggests that everyone has their own demons and at the final hour they must be faced.

7 **the Arch Fear** Again death is personified as that which is feared most, developing the earlier impressions of apprehension and anxiety. How successful is Browning in presenting this idea?

11 **guerdon** recompense or reward.

12 The line suggests that a release and liberation can be attained, but only after the battle with one's fears has been won.

15–18 The language in these lines suggests a desire to experience every moment of dying, as of living; *let me taste the whole of it* suggests that full awareness and sensory perception should be paramount at the moment of death.

19 **Bear the brunt** This alliterative phrase suggests the difficulty of enduring and braving the unknown.

pay glad life's arrears   Christian ideas are alluded to here as Browning suggests that the dying have to account for what they have done with their lives.

21–3   The process of dying, passing through fear and pain, is again described using the pathetic fallacy of *the elements' rage*.

24–6   The mood of the poem gradually changes here as the tone becomes calm, and once again Christian ideas are used to suggest the *peace* and *light* that are hoped for after death.

27–8   The last lines of the poem movingly insist that after death one is assured of reunion with lost loved ones. The poet addresses his late wife as *soul of my soul* and concludes with the belief that *I shall clasp thee again*.

Apparent Failure

This poem begins with an assertive response to a statement in a *Paris Newspaper*, as Browning reflects on his visit to this city *Seven years since*, to see the christening of Napoleon III's son. The focus of the poem is on the walk he took afterwards along the banks of the Seine. It was here that he happened upon a morgue in which the bodies of those who had drowned in the river Seine were kept while they awaited identification. A newspaper report that this building was threatened with demolition prompted the poem.

Browning's belief that he will save the building by the very act of writing about it gives life to his poem. He uses the poem to explore his philosophy of the imperfect (see page 175) and his insistence that having a consciousness of failure is in fact a measure of success.

3   **your Prince**   Louis Napoleon, the son of Napoleon III, born in 1856.

6   **the Seine-side**   the riverbank that runs through central Paris.

7   **Congress**   the Congress of Paris, which took place in 1856 to agree the terms of peace following the Crimean War.
Gortschakoff   Russia's representative at the Congress of Paris.

8   **Cavour**   representative at the Congress of Paris for

Piedmont, who had ambitions (which he later realized) to unite Italy.

Buol Austria's representative at the Congress of Paris (Austria at this time ruled the Italian peninsula).

10 **Doric little Morgue** The morgue was designed in the *Doric* style of classical Greek architecture.

12 **Petrarch's Vaucluse** The town of Vaucluse in south-eastern France was for a time the home of the famous Italian poet Petrarch (1304–74).

Sorgue river that rises in Vaucluse.

14 **debt** i.e. the necessity or obligation to visit a famous place.

18 **No Briton's to be balked** no British person is to be deterred.

19 **silent gazers** those who stare like voyeurs. What tone do you feel Browning is adopting here?

25 **copper couch** metal table where the dead are laid out.

32 **Sacred from touch** This implies that the coat, like the man who owned it, is now safely out of the clutches of those who would defile it.

34 **tenanted** The word suggests that life on earth is merely borrowed rather than owned, and human beings are given a fixed term in which to live on it.

35 **Some arch** This suggests the men were homeless and lived on the streets exposed to the elements.

38 **Buonaparte** military and political leader of France whose actions shaped the history of early nineteenth-century Europe.

39 **Tuileries** the imperial palace in Paris.

43 **leveller** one who belonged to a political movement demanding equality, extended voting rights and religious tolerance.

46–7 **red in vain,/ Or black** This refers to the *red* and *black* of the gambling game roulette. Browning turns to speculating on the passions and vices that have brought the men to ruin and suicide. How sympathetic do you feel Browning is to those who have taken their own lives?

58 **My own hope** What do you make of the *hope* expressed in the final stanza?

63 **what God blessed once** Does the poet include every human being in this blessing, and therefore in his *hope*? Compare line 28.

Interpretations

During his lifetime, Robert Browning's work was greeted with varying critical responses. His early work was not well received, and even the publication of *Men and Women*, the collection now considered to contain some of Browning's greatest poems, was regarded as obscure; one critic went so far as to say it was a 'wilderness of mist and of sand'. Browning felt that he had created works that deserved a wide readership, and although he admitted that the way in which he had created his poetry was new and challenging, he wrote to his friend John Forster: 'The manner will be newer than the matter' and 'I hope to be listened to, this time'.

This section will look at different interpretations of Browning's poetry. Today, he is generally regarded as one of the greatest poets of the Victorian period. He is revered for his radical approach to poetry, and especially for what he achieved with the dramatic monologue form, weaving into it his love of art, music, history, and of course Italy. His poetry is admired for its energy, and its varieties of mood, form and subject matter.

Themes and ideas

Art

It is well known that Browning loved Italy, his adopted country, and had a particular interest in Italian Renaissance art. He was fascinated by painting and sculpture, and it was not enough for him simply to admire others but he spent many days modelling clay and making busts, then breaking them. In *Andrea del Sarto* and *Fra Lippo Lippi*, Browning describes the technicalities of painting, concerning himself with the surfaces, materials and colours that painters used. But although the technical aspects of art interested him, for Browning the vital issue was that art expressed a love of living things, and it this idea that he explores in *Fra Lippo Lippi*. In Browning's poem, Lippi is an artist who is awake to the variety, power and beauty of life in the flesh, and in consequence – in Browning's view – the soul. The opposite is true of the speaker in *Andrea del Sarto*, who feels that in his faultless paintings he misses the fire and the energy of life. In *Pictor Ignotus*, the speaker withdraws from the world and confines his art to the *cloisters* and *sanctuary*.

Browning's work can be seen as a kind of poetic canvas in which he uses colour and imagery to create characters and scenes. He also had a love of the Gothic or grotesque, and when he explores this in his poetry he creates an energy that takes its own form. In 'Childe Roland to the Dark Tower Came', Browning moves away from conventional descriptions of the beauties of nature to create a picture of a wilderness, offering the reader a vivid engagement with a wasteland that has a paradoxical beauty and power of its own. Nature in its raw state is brought vividly to life as Childe Roland asks:

> What made those holes and rents
> In the dock's harsh swarth leaves, bruised as to baulk
> All hope of greenness?
>
> (69–71)

Here as in all of his writing Browning uses his love of the richness, colours and textures of art to give life to his descriptions.

Activity

Explore the ways in which ideas about art are presented in *Fra Lippo Lippi* and *Andrea del Sarto*.

Discussion

Fra Lippo Lippi is first presented to the reader as a pleasure-loving monk who has been lured outside at night by the sound of merriment in the street. Throughout the poem Browning not only develops the contradictions in the situation and character of this individual, through the use of the dramatic monologue, but also gives a vivid sense of Lippi's eye as a painter. He is inspired to paint images of the ordinary people he meets – he calls for chalk to sketch the faces of his captors. 'Ordinary' people, to him, all have something extraordinary about them, which he longs to capture and preserve in the form of portraits.

However, Browning explores issues in the way art is received, as painting that reflects everyday life is rejected by the Prior and the learned men who insist that *the souls of men* (183) cannot be revealed through paintings that offer clear likenesses of individual people. These critics have a distaste for human flesh, dismissing it as *perishable clay* (180) and Lippi's work as the *devil's-game* (178). It is through Lippi's response that Browning poses questions concerning what can be defined as beautiful and meaningful. If beauty is created through depicting the physical world, does this prevent an artist from addressing deeper, spiritual meanings? Lippi insists that when looking at art *you'll find the soul you have missed,/Within yourself* (219–220), suggesting that it is possible to respond in this way to all great art. Thus Browning argues through the voice of Lippi in favour of the realism in Renaissance art, asserting that *God made it all!* (285).

In Andrea del Sarto, Browning depicts an artist who has lost faith in his work, a man who sees his paintings as proficient and even faultless, but lacking *the play, the insight and the stretch* (116) that other artists can achieve. Andrea acknowledges that although his rival Raphael's work might not be faultless, *its soul is right* (113), in contrast to his own work. However, Browning shows through various images that Andrea has an imaginative and sensuous engagement with the world, and most importantly with the woman he loves. Andrea describes her hand as *a woman of itself* (21), and a visual representation of their love is developed through the image of Andrea's hand being *the man's bared breast she curls inside* (22).

A Filippo Lippi painting of the Virgin and Child, painted in the 1450s

Through the character of Andrea del Sarto, Browning explores the issues of self-doubt and artistic inspiration. The reader is presented with the paradoxical situation of a man who acknowledges his own skill in painting, saying he *can do with my pencil what I know,/ What I see... when I say, perfectly,/ I do not boast* (60–64) yet who sees something lacking in his work and acknowledges that he depends on the (unreliable) love of his wife for inspiration; he suggests that if she had given him *soul*, he could have achieved what Raphael achieved. Here Browning touches on the importance of having a sensitive and responsive muse (in Greek mythology, a muse is a goddess or spirit who inspires the creation of literature and other arts). On the one hand the artist's wife, Lucrezia, is the motivating factor in his work, but on the other her lack of support and her financial extravagance have robbed him of any true inspiration and contributed to his fall from grace.

Browning develops Andrea's character through the use of colour imagery; his feelings of worthlessness are reflected in the *common greyness* that *silvers everything* (35), resulting in his life being *toned down* (39). Thus Browning reminds the reader that his character is an artist who sees the world in terms of colour tones and shades.

In both of these poems Browning explores the complexity of the artist's imagination and human fallibility, while raising philosophical questions about the nature of art and its reception.

Pictor Ignotus is another dramatic monologue in which Browning addresses the issue of the relationship between material success and great art. It offers a further picture of a painter who sees himself as a failure in some respects, but in contrast to Andrea del Sarto, who has embraced material rewards, the speaker in this poem has retreated from the world. He seems a rather weak and timid individual, and condemns himself when he speaks of the *monotonous* (58) works that he produces. Browning, however, with his mastery of the form of the dramatic monologue, is able to present the reader with the complexity of human emotions and experience, and there is pathos in the speaker's acknowledgement that *My heart sinks, as... I paint* (58). He may be attempting to justify himself in his assertion that *At least no merchant traffics in my heart* (62), but the reader is left in no doubt that the painter is aware that he has failed to use *all my gift/ Of fires from God* (5–6).

Browning's aim in all three of the monologues spoken by Renaissance painters is to depict the men complete with their failings and the compromises they have had to make. The speaker in *Pictor Ignotus* justifies his failures by claiming to reject the commercialization of art, but he also suggests that he realizes he has wasted his talents and that his creative spirit has been quenched. It seems that he, like his pictures, will *moulder* (67) and *die* (69) in obscurity. He may claim, as the poem closes, that worldly success and *praise* are transitory, but Browning leaves the reader in no doubt that these rationalizations cannot obscure the truth that he has buried his talents and passions in *The sanctuary's gloom* (63).

Italy and England

Browning described Italy as 'my university', and it was in this country that he wrote most of his great works. He was inspired by Florence and Venice with their great works of art. However, what he celebrates in the second stanza of '*De Gustibus* –' is not the high culture of Italy but its magnificent scenery and its people, both of which he felt exemplified the energy and spirit of Italy. In this poem Browning describes his feelings for Italy, *the land of lands* (20), in terms of a love affair. Italy underwent turbulent political changes during his time in the country, and the anarchic spirit that characterizes the nation in his poem is personified through the presentation of the young girl. The quiet, gentle and rather sleepy nature of the English, metaphorically presented through the description of the lovers in the country lane in the first stanza, is contrasted with the passion and intensity of the Italian people inspired by their rugged countryside and the power of the Mediterranean sun.

In *Love Among the Ruins* Browning again uses the landscape of Italy to explore love, desire and passion, but in this poem he fuses the past with the present and contrasts the corruption of the urban, political world with the intensity and urgency of love in a rural landscape.

By contrast *Up at a Villa – Down in the City* presents the reader with a picture of the bustle of city life in nineteenth-century Italy and a glimpse of the realities of life in the countryside. Rather than being a vehicle for a simple celebration of the delights of city living, the views of the speaker are gently satirized; the anti-liberal politics of the speaker, for example, are in complete opposition to those of Browning.

Activity

Consider the contrasts Browning presents in *Up at a Villa – Down in the City* between life in the country and life in town. In your discussion, consider the paradoxical presentation of both locations.

Discussion

The speaker describes his life in the country villa as dull and uneventful, and dislikes the peaceful landscape he describes, but Browning seemingly subverts this. In the fifth and sixth stanzas he offers a picture of a tranquil life in the Italian countryside that the reader may notice has its own colours, textures and charms, and seems to offer positive alternatives to the animation of the city. The poem is characterized by repeated contrasts between the restless energy of city life – which has many attractive aspects but where even the image of the Virgin Mary is vulgarly adorned in a *pink gauze gown, all spangles* (52) – and the natural beauty of the countryside where *The wild tulip... blows out its great red bell* (24). Unlike '*De Gustibus –,*' however, the poem does acknowledge some of the harsh realities of living in the countryside. The speaker offers images of the changing seasons both in the town and in the country, and we are reminded that, although the entertainments of the town may seem shallow, life in the country is often hard. The speaker reinforces this idea even more powerfully by claiming to gloss over the worst aspects – *I spare you the months of the fever and chill* (37) – and the reader is left to reflect on the balance between being part of a lively society and enjoying tranquillity, between human creativeness and natural beauty, and between different types of comfort and discomfort.

Browning also loved the English countryside, and he celebrates the beauty of England in *Home-Thoughts, from Abroad*. Here he brings to life the glory of an English springtime, as it is seen in the imagination of a person who is living far away. He praises the beauty of the humble buttercup, favourably contrasting it with the *gaudy* flowers of the Mediterranean (20). In these poems we see Browning's love for both countries; although he spent most of his later life in Italy, he clearly felt a great love for his country of origin. The sentiments expressed in these poems perhaps reflect his changing moods and circumstances.

Activity

Consider how Browning engages the reader through vivid descriptions of the natural world in a poem of your choice.

Discussion

In the second stanza of *'De Gustibus –'*, the reader is presented with a vivid picture of all that Browning found so captivating about Italy. The language is rich and varied and the poem works as a series of images that capture the beauty and energy of the country. Browning paints a picture in words as he describes *a castle, precipice-encurled,/ In a gash of the wind-grieved Apennine* (15–16). The compound adjectives, *precipice-encurled* and *wind-grieved*, suggest that nature is wild and untamed, and there is a sense of nature dominating the works of human beings.

Meeting at Night offers a powerful depiction of the passions of a lover as he travels across sea and land to meet his lady. In this poem Browning evokes sexual desire through his description of the life and power of the sea and the way the lover drives the boat into the cove and onto the sand. The energy and urgency of the lover are reflected in vivid images of the dark and tempestuous water. In the opening description of *The grey sea and the long black land;/ And the yellow half-moon large and low*, Browning applies his artist's palette to his poetry.

Love

Many of Browning's poems address the subject of love in its different guises and moods. At a personal level, Browning seems to have believed that the experience of love can be an epiphany – a moment of sudden understanding, like a divine revelation. His love affair with Elizabeth Barrett resulted in a life-long attachment and happy marriage; his first letter to her, written on 10 January 1845 in admiration of her poems before they had even met, alludes to the idea of love as an epiphanic moment.

> I do, as I say, love these books with all my heart – and I love you too: do you know I was once not very far from seeing – really seeing you? Mr Kenyon said to me one morning 'Would you like to see Miss Barrett?' – then he went to announce me, – then he returned... you were too unwell – and now it is years ago – and I feel as at some untoward passage in my travels – as if I had been close, so close, to some world's-wonder in chapel or crypt, only a screen to push and I might have entered, but there was some slight... so it now seems... slight and just-sufficient bar to admission; and the half-opened door shut, and I went home my thousands of miles, and the sight was never to be!

Browning's allusion to 'some world's-wonder in chapel or crypt' alerts us not only to his passion for art but to his belief that his admiration for Elizabeth Barrett offered him a sense of something sublime.

However, Browning did not limit himself to writing about successful romantic love, and his poems often explore the darker side of love. He writes about its sometimes transitory nature, about jealousy and obsession, about destructive and even violent love; about love that is characterized by morbid lack of fulfilment, love as a quest for perfection, and love of country. In Browning's treatment of love we are reminded of Theseus's comment in *A Midsummer Night's Dream*: 'The lunatic, the lover, and the poet/ Are of imagination all compact' (V.i.7–8).

In *Porphyria's Lover* and *My Last Duchess*, Browning explores the disturbed psychology of a man who seeks to destroy the individuality of a woman and eventually kills her in order to retain power over her. Here we see love corrupted by self-delusion and the need to control others; both of the male protagonists in these poems seem to be characterized by the need for sadistic domination of women. Porphyria is murdered because her lover finds it intolerable that she seems unwilling to give up everything for his love. He strangles her in an attempt to preserve for ever a moment when he finally seems to be in control of her: *That moment she was mine, mine, fair,/ Perfectly pure and good* (36–7). He acknowledges that she *worshipped me* (33), but his insecurity leads him to desire complete domination. Here we see love as a form of madness in a character who shows a chilling arrogance, going so far as to challenge God's power.

Similarly, in *My Last Duchess* love is a destructive force; here the speaker destroys his Duchess because he cannot tolerate her capacity to respond deeply to the world and to other people. It is as if he is so empty within himself that he needs to consume the whole personality of another, and in consequence he cannot accept her delight in anyone or anything other than himself. Here Browning explores the nature of jealousy, as it seems that the Duke believes his wife's capacity for love and delight is so generous it is a kind of infidelity.

Activity

Looking closely at *My Last Duchess* and *Porphyria's Lover*, consider how Browning explores obsessive and destructive love.

Discussion

Porphyria's Lover opens with a setting that appears troubled. Through the use of the pathetic fallacy, the *sullen wind* that *did its worst to vex the lake* reflects the troubled state of mind of the speaker. In contrast, the language used to describe Porphyria is gentle, almost ethereal, as she is seen to glide into the room and *shut the cold out and the storm* (7). The imagery used to describe the transformation she creates in the cottage alerts the reader to the warmth and passion of the young woman. Literally, she lights a fire, but the word *Blaze* and the fact that her actions *warm* the cottage (9) associate her with passion and sensuality. This is compounded by the description of the way in which she discards her outer clothing and loosens her hair, and the verbs *Withdrew, laid... by,* and *let... fall* (11–13) create a seductive atmosphere.

The warm, intimate and trusting behaviour of Porphyria contrasts, however, with the voice of the speaker, as his criticisms of what he terms her *pride* and *vainer ties* (24) reveal his lack of trust, his insecurity and his obsessive fear that she will not be his and his alone *for ever* (25). It is not jealousy but an obsession with securing the lover *for ever* that motivates his violent act, as the speaker realizes that although she may appear proud, nevertheless *Porphyria worshipped me* (33). Browning here touches on the issue explored in *The Last Ride Together* and *Two in the Campagna*, that of capturing a special moment for eternity. Here, the speaker resolves to fix the moment by murdering his lover.

In her death the speaker has attained supremacy and what he feared before – her pride and her laughing eyes – now contain no threat. Browning develops the idea of dominance and the desire for absolute power through the speaker's insistence that his lover is now passive and *this time my shoulder bore/ Her head* (50–51). In an even darker twist the speaker justifies his actions by insisting that he has given Porphyria the opportunity to satisfy her *utmost will* (53) and belong to him completely. The poem thus explores the complexity of self-love and vanity as well as the madness created by obsessive love; the speaker insists that his lover's head, which he now supports, is free from *all it scorned... /And I, its love, am gained instead!* (54–55).

In this poem a pro-active and passionate woman is ultimately tamed by a male who begins by seeming helpless, but finally attains dominance. In a Victorian society that feared or refused to acknowledge female sexuality, the overt passion of Porphyria could be deemed unacceptable and deserving of repression. Browning shows this idea taken to its horrifying conclusion, and hints at its madness.

In *My Last Duchess* Browning draws on his interest in Italy and Renaissance art as he explores the contradictions in the character of the Duke. He is a man who has an aesthetic appreciation of art and yet behaves with murderous cruelty in his personal relationships. The poem opens with a dispassionate comment from the Duke about the painting of his wife, immediately distancing him from any emotional attachment to her. As the conversation between the Duke and his visitor progresses, the reader becomes increasingly aware that the Duke disapproved of his wife's behaviour – in fact of her personality. Once again Browning shows the reader a man whose own insecurities lead him to see faults in others. The Duke asserts that his wife had *A heart... too soon made glad* (22) and he clearly feels threatened by anyone or anything that appeared to please her. Here Browning explores not just jealousy but an obsessive self-importance, which is developed as the character reveals his conceit and arrogance. He mentions his *nine-hundred-years-old name* (33) and his surprise that his wife did not appear to rank his *gift* of this name to her above everything else in her life. The Duke's egotistical pride is further developed as he insists that he would not *stoop* (42–43) to alert his wife to his disapproval. Once again Browning creates a scenario in which the active and responsive female must be silenced and, in a chilling climax, the speaker boasts of how *I gave commands;/ Then all smiles stopped together* (45–46).

On the one hand it is possible to read this poem as an exploration of obsessive self-love and to view the speaker as a cold, calculating murderer who shows no remorse. Alternatively one might argue that as in *Porphyria's Lover* Browning is exposing the fears of Victorian society concerning female sexuality, as here again the reader is presented with the murder of a young woman whose fault lies in her attractiveness and her capacity for pleasure.

It is not just male protagonists who show an extreme form of jealousy. In *The Laboratory* Browning explores the psychology of a woman who is driven by jealousy to seek violent revenge on a rival. Once again we see the destructive power of self-obsessed love, and the lengths to which such troubled people will go in an attempt to ease their pain and confusion. The female speaker of the poem is clearly disturbed and exploitative, but being a woman she is relatively powerless; this poem is a study of someone seeking to take revenge by stealth rather than direct violence.

The Pre-Raphaelite artist Dante Gabriel Rossetti painted this water-colour inspired by *The Laboratory*

Behind the shocking actions in these poems are the powerful feelings of sexual passion. The Victorian period was character-ized by censorship of overt depictions of sexuality, and so allu-sions to desire had to be veiled. In *Meeting at Night* Browning uses rich and sensuous language to describe the speaker's quest to meet his lover. In contrast, however, in the short poem *Parting at Morning* Browning depicts the transitory nature of love and the conflict between the (characteristically male?) desire for engagement with the world and the insular, all-enveloping inti-macy of the night before.

Browning explores failure in love in such poems as *The Last Ride Together* as well as his paired poems *Meeting at Night, Parting at Morning* and *Love in a Life, Life in a Love*.

Activity

How does Browning explore failure in love in *Love in a Life* and *Life in a Love*?

Discussion

In *Love in a Life* and *Life in a Love* Browning introduces the idea of love as a quest for the unattainable. (See page 181 for a discussion of Browning's use of the 'quest' theme.) The lover's pursuit is endless and unfulfilled, and there is a note of frustration as well as unfailing fascination with the loved one. The repetition in the opening line of *Love in a Life* suggests a sense of desperation. This is compounded by the admission in *Life in a Love* that *the chace takes up one's life, that's all* (15). Hence it seems that it is the pursuit, rather than the realiza-tion of experience, that drives the speaker of the poem. A type of pleasure can be attained from a lack of resolution; for can fulfilment ever match idealized desire? The *chace* offers an ongoing sense of possibility, and it this that ultimately shapes the speaker's mood.

Through the pairing of these two poems and others like them, Browning engages with the complexity of human emotion. Throughout *Love in a Life* there is a reiterated insistence on the idea that the two lovers inhabit the same space, not just literally, as in sharing a home, but in the mind and thoughts. Thus when the speaker asserts *Heart, fear nothing, for, heart, thou shalt find her* (4), there is a sense in which the lover believes that he and his mistress are as one despite her apparent elusiveness. Hence the quest is as much about seeking the physical body of the woman as it is about the merging of two minds.

Browning uses the image of the house as a metaphor for the mind, and the poem comes to a climax as the lover asserts his lucklessness: *Range the wide house from the wing to the centre./ Still the same chance! she goes out as I enter* (12–13). However, the poem ends on a note of optimism as the lover remains undefeated in spirit and sees the search as a challenge that will ultimately offer as-yet-unexpressed possibilities.

The matching poem *Life in a Love* begins in a rather confrontational mood, as the lover suggests through a rhetorical question and answer (*Escape me?/ Never*) that his lover will not be able to fly from him. However, this optimistic assertion is soon replaced by the dejection with which the lover accepts that *Though I do my best I shall scarce succeed* (10). Browning uses the idea of courtly love to explore the complexity of the male mind when in pursuit of an unattainable lover. Browning's use of the word *fault*, when the speaker asserts *My life is a fault at last* (8), is interesting; on the one hand this suggests failure, but on the other hand the word *fault* is a hunting term and it gives the poem a darker tone as the lover appears to celebrate the idea of the pursuit. Browning touches here on the idea of obsessive love, which he explores in more detail in his dramatic monologues. In this poem the reader is presented with the turbulent and changing emotions of a lover who defines his life in terms of the pursuit of love; the loss of one hope is replaced almost immediately with *a new one, straight to the self-same mark* (19). Thus it can be argued that Browning redefines the idea of failure in terms of the pleasure that is to be found in a lack of resolution and the perpetual desire for the unattainable.

The Last Ride Together is one of the poems in which Browning explores the issue of unrequited love, and how failure can be redefined as success.

Activity

Look closely at *The Last Ride Together* and consider the issues it raises about love.

Discussion

This poem opens with a sense of failure and acceptance of this as the speaker acknowledges that *nothing all my love avails* (3). However, the focus turns to the pleasure to be gained from *one more last ride* (11) and the language becomes increasingly sensual as the speaker seems to gain new life from the expectation of delight in the ride. The description of nature acts as a reflection of his mind, as in the alliterative *All billowy-bosomed, over-bowed/ By many benedictions* (24–25). The word *benedictions* implies that the beauty of the *western cloud* is a kind of blessing, and this is taken up again when the speaker begins to define his pleasure not as pleasure of the flesh but of the spirit; he alludes to the glory to be gained from this ride together, as *flesh must fade for heaven was here!* (31). Browning develops this idea of a spiritual experience or a moment of epiphany, as the speaker does not describe his physical position next to his lover but instead refers to his soul, which *Smoothed itself out* (35).

It is at this point in the poem that Browning introduces the question of the nature of success and failure, and whether the former is even possible in human lives, as the speaker questions, *Fail I alone, in words and deeds?/ Why, all men strive and who succeeds?* (45–46). Thus the speaker celebrates the immediacy of the moment and the glory of the ride in contrast to the fragile nature of the fulfilment and glory that can be gained by worldly success: *My riding is better, by their leave* (66).

The voice of the speaker poses a philosophical question as to what would ensue if *fate* gave the lover his *bliss* (89–90) on earth through his love being returned. This question is ultimately resolved in a celebration of the pleasure to be gained in anticipating bliss, both in heaven and connected to earthly love, both of which still remain *beyond this ride* (99). Thus Browning returns to the idea that failure in love can in itself be a form of success as these two lovers are in the prime of their lives and *life's flower* (103) seems to be within their grasp. The speaker questions whether this experience, fixed as it is within this moment in time, could be an anticipation of bliss or even heaven in itself. The poem ends with an affirmation that bliss is anticipation rather than the fulfilment of desire, and with a repetition of the present-tense verb *ride*, which emphasizes a continuing present. Thus failure and disappointment are negated by a celebration of the moment, fixed for *eternity* as the speaker affirms they have the potential to *Ride, ride together, for ever ride*.

Two in the Campagna is another poem in which Browning addresses the issue of longing to capture a moment of perfect bliss, and coming to terms with the fact that it is impossible.

Activity

What aspects of success and failure in love does Browning address in *Two in the Campagna*?

Discussion

The lovers in *Two in the Campagna* appear to be in harmony, yet the speaker is troubled. The poem begins with a direct, conversational address to the speaker's lover: *I wonder do you feel to-day...* But there is a mixture of tenses as the voice considers a moment that has passed – one in which he *touched a thought* (6), and his memories appear to be linked to the physical objects over which his attention is moving. The speaker reflects on the beauty of the achieved *good minute* (50); this is balanced by his yearning and his attempt to *Catch your soul's warmth* (48). However, the moment is transient and as the *rose* is plucked, so the speaker loses that sense of connection.

The poem is framed by the way thought processes move between associations, memories and desires, and this associative process fixes upon things that are both growing and dead: *The yellowing fennel, run to seed/... Some old tomb's ruin* (12, 14). Like the fleeting experience itself, the thought process is constantly escaping from control. The speaker calls to his lover to *Help me to hold it!* (11) but it moves on, escaping definition, just like a transient glimpse of paradise reached for and then lost. Though he seeks to fix thoughts and experiences, the elusiveness of both is caught in the words *Off again* (57), as the speaker acknowledges his inability to capture any moment or thought in time. Browning suggests that the very nature of thought prevents moments of experience, however precious, from being *primal* (28), unlike the *forms* of nature, because human beings can only comprehend them through the power of the imagination. It is possible, therefore, to *discern.../ Infinite passion* (58–59), but not to contain it, so the lover must accept *the pain/ Of finite hearts that yearn* (59–60).

In terms of Browning's philosophy of the imperfect (see page 175), this can be viewed in a positive light as the lover continues to yearn and to quest for that vision of the infinite. Although this can never be attained, it is the pursuit itself that defines victory, as the lover continues to long for the loved one and can never experience failure or disappointment. See Note to line 106 of *The Last Ride Together*, pages 132–133.

Exploring the idea of dreams and visions in his love poetry allowed Browning to be more explicit about sexual love than was usual in writing of the time. For example, *Women and Roses* takes the form of the record of a dream. It is undoubtedly an erotic dream, but it is projected into the past and the future as well as the present. The male speaker attempts to determine which of the three groups of women is *dearest* to him, and the language is characterized by sensual imagery. There seems to be an attempt throughout the poem to possess and contain these women, who tantalize the speaker in his dream. However, he is unable to fix any of the three *roses* either in his art or in his life. Nevertheless, the fact that Browning presents the women as continuing to circle the *red-rose tree* suggests that the desirable vision they represent is unchanging and eternal, even though particular manifestations of it – the three roses – are subject to change and decay. Here, then, love is presented as an erotic desire within the male psyche that can never be satisfied, and the tone is not one of ecstasy but of frustration.

Activity

In what ways does Browning present women in *Women and Roses*?

Discussion

Women are presented symbolically, through the image of the rose circling the tree of the speaker's imagination. The language is sensual and at times erotic, as the speaker alludes to quenching his desires *at a plunge… Eyes in your eyes, lips on your lips!* (31–32). There are also images of control; as he conjures an image of a woman as yet *unborn* (38), the speaker plays with the idea of being the artist who has the power to shape her *to his mind* (47). However, the poem concludes in a tone of disappointment and frustration as the figures continue to dance around the tree but seem impossible to contain. The male speaker is left questing for the unattainable.

There is no female voice in the poem, and it is possible to read it as a flight of male fantasy. An alternative reading might suggest that Browning is attacking Victorian male attitudes towards female sexuality, as the speaker is only able explore his fantasies within the context of a dream. The need to possess and contain the women, albeit within the artist's frame, suggests the speaker's fear of the endless desire *to possess, and be possessed* (20). The fact that the poem concludes with the speaker's acceptance that he is to be forever yearning can perhaps be read as offering relief rather than frustration, in that the excitement of the quest is what is important rather than the satisfaction of fulfilled desire.

See page 204 for a discussion of feminist readings of Browning's poetry.

In *A Woman's Last Word* Browning unusually offers the reader the voice of a woman. Throughout the poem Browning represents the experience of love as a paradise or Garden of Eden, and it is the *wild words* (5) that destroy happiness like the serpent in the garden. The lovers are presented through the image of birds *In debate* (7) who are unaware of the danger posed by their arguments; their relationship is threatened just as the *Hawk on bough* (8) threatens the birds. The happiness of love is associated with paradise, but disputes between the lovers distance them from awareness of the imaginative or spiritual world evoked in the poem.

As suggested in the Notes (see page 113) there are different ways of reading this poem. It can be argued that the woman speaker recognizes that to be able to grasp their paradise, the two must be as one, *Cheek on cheek* (12). A feminist reading (see page 204) might suggest that Browning presents the woman as one who must be moulded by the man, as in stanzas 6 and 7, otherwise she will remain forever spiritually adrift.

Activity

Consider alternative ways of reading Browning's presentation of the woman in *A Woman's Last Word*.

Discussion

Throughout the poem the speaker's tone appears to be conciliatory, and she seems humbled and sorrowful. The fragmented phrasing of the opening stanza seems to reflect her mood as she fretfully asks for all to *be as before* (3). However, perhaps her wish that her lover does not reply to her but that he should *Only sleep* (4) may be a way of empowering herself, as he is encouraged to abandon thought and be lulled to sleep in her arms. If we accept this reading, then her later offer to be subsumed by the male identity, *Laying flesh and spirit/ In thy hands* (31–32), may be seen as a way of exploiting her apparent vulnerability in order to attain the emotional calm she desires. If read in this way, the speaker may be similar to the female speaker in *The Laboratory*, who exploits the apothecary to achieve her ends. It can be argued that Browning is presenting an image of a temptress who, having buried *sorrow/ Out of sight* (35–36), *Must a little weep* (37) and then, secure in the knowledge of her victory can, *fall asleep.../ Loved* (39–40).

Alternatively, it can be suggested that Browning presents another form of male fantasy, that of the complete self-abasement of the woman. In this reading it is the silent male who is the victor, as the woman seeks security, asking to be folded *With thine arm* (24). The use of the word *fold* suggests the idea of being enveloped and enclosed within the male world. The woman seems no longer able to define herself but must be taught to *speak thy speech* (27) and *Think thy thought* (28). Her humility extends to acknowledging that, should her lover require it, she is prepared to offer all of herself, both *flesh and spirit* (31). There is a sense here of accepting that the wild bird must be tamed, and must *contend no more* (1) with the man if she is to have any hope of happiness. In this reading Browning seems to suggest that the woman is deliberately choosing to be *Foolish* (38) in submitting to the man in order to gain a glimpse of paradise.

Love of country is another type of love that interested Browning, as we have seen in '*De Gustibus –*', where the poet's attraction to Italy is treated as a love affair – *Open my heart and you will see/ Graved inside of it, 'Italy'* (43–44) – and *Home-Thoughts, from Abroad* (see pages 155–157).

In *The Patriot* Browning offers a rather ambiguous engagement with the love of one's country, as he explores the capricious nature of human loyalties. The voice of the poem is that of a man who appears to have devoted himself to the people of his country, and who retains a sense of optimism and belief in God's mercy despite being led to execution.

The poem opens with a retrospective view as the speaker describes his reception by the people a year ago; the first stanza describes how they welcomed him with *roses*, *myrtle* and *flags* and hailed him as a hero. The poem is characterized by a kaleidoscope of visual and auditory images, both of the glorious welcome he received then and the situation in the 'now' of the poem. Browning contrasts the scene where the returning hero is glorified with the one where, as a condemned man, he is scorned before his execution. As in many of his dramatic monologues, Browning thus explores the darker side of human nature. The fickleness of popular support is emphasized, as the poem contains no explanation for either the speaker's status as a hero or his fall from grace; we are simply shown that when he loses favour, the *harvest* (14) of his efforts on behalf of his *loving friends* (12) is to be his execution, for what are considered to be his *year's misdeeds* (25). The irony in the word *harvest* relates to the capricious way in which rewards are given out in this world, and this is reinforced by the tone of the poem as it moves from a celebratory mood to one of gravity and solemnity. Nevertheless, the speaker maintains a sense of optimism in that he looks to heaven for a sounder judgement, and in the final line he asserts *'Tis God shall repay: I am safer so.*

As with many of Browning's poems that offer a critical engagement with social values, *The Patriot* is set in a foreign land and in the past; this is signalled by archaic language such as *Alack* (11) and *trow* (20). In this way Browning distances his writing from contemporary society; he avoids directly challenging Victorian attitudes and values but is able to make more general observations on the transience of fame and glory and the savage ingratitude that humankind is capable of.

Activity

Consider the ways in which the speaker in *The Patriot* is presented as a man 'more sinned against than sinning'.

Discussion

Browning's choice of the dramatic monologue offers the reader a first-person narrative, and in consequence invites us to empathize with the speaker's perception of events. The celebratory tone that characterizes the first two stanzas serves to create pathos as the speaker moves on to reveal his fall from favour and his imminent death.

The use of the term *crowd* (7) suggests a multitude of people being swept away by emotion and acting as one rather than making individual judgements. At the beginning they seem in awe of the speaker and it could be argued that the way in which the narrator describes his reception echoes the welcome given to Christ as he rode into Jerusalem on a donkey, a week before his crucifixion, as described in Mark 11:1–11. To develop the analogy, the speaker becomes like the persecuted Christ as the tone and mood of the poem become darker; the speaker reveals that he is approaching the place of execution and *A rope cuts both my wrists behind;/ And I think, by the feel, my forehead bleeds* (22–23).

The poem doesn't reveal what the *misdeeds* (25) of the speaker are, but the tone of the poem encourages the reader to believe that his punishment is undeserved, just as possibly the extravagance of his welcome may have been. In the final lines the Patriot looks to God for a fairer judgement and for mercy, just as Christ did on the cross. Thus Browning presents the reader with a man who is to be sacrificed because he has fallen from favour despite having *leaped at the sun/ To give it my loving friends to keep!* (11–12). He, like Christ, is to die like a common criminal and be humiliated at the point of death, as onlookers stare from their windows to gain *the best of the sight* (18) of his demise.

The Lost Leader is an interesting exploration of the relationship between a leader and the country he loves, as it contains an attack on William Wordsworth (See Notes page 94). The tone of disparagement that characterizes the poem reveals Browning's horror at those who sacrifice their principles in return for a privileged position in society.

Activity

Consider the ways in which Browning presents Wordsworth, and more generally all those who choose to join the established elite rather than follow the more difficult road of promoting liberal causes.

Discussion

The Lost Leader takes the form of an emotional outburst by a follower let down by his hero. The speaker seems almost unable to believe Wordsworth's betrayal of *We that had loved him so, followed him, honoured him* (9), which is felt like a bereavement. The dismissive statement *let him never come back to us*! (25) is qualified by the tone of disappointment in the speaker's assertion that there can never be *glad confident morning again* (28). In these lines the speaker seems to consider the idea of the possible restoration of the leader's position, but convinces himself and perhaps an audience that this could never happen.

Browning despised those whom he considered to be traitors to a noble cause. In *'Childe Roland to the Dark Tower Came'* we are alerted to Browning's celebration of those who continue a quest against all the odds (see page 181); Childe Roland rises to the challenge of his terrifying ordeal, in contrast to other knights who fall from grace. The tone of *The Lost Leader*, however, is not just one of denunciation but also of sadness for what has been lost.

The poem does not name Wordsworth or state in explicit terms which cause he is deserting. The reader might question how much a writer such as Wordsworth has an obligation to his audience in terms of his political principles, but the impassioned tone of the poem reinforces the sense of the speaker being badly let down, and it is an uncompromising expression of emotion arising from political principles.

Women's position in society

In Browning's time, social stability depended on a dominant patriarchal culture, one in which women fulfilled a domestic role and acted as aids to men. John Ruskin, a leading writer and critic of the time who championed Browning's work, argued in favour of female education, not because it would liberate women but to enable each to 'help her husband by what she knows' (*Sesame and Lilies*, 1865). Women who did not conform to the expected role were seen as threatening, and likely to turn the world upside down.

Women who sought education and showed a determination to develop their lives outside of marriage and motherhood were labelled freakish, and many scientists argued that their behaviour would lead to sickness, sterility and ultimately degeneration of the human race. Male anxiety was often focused on fertility, and doctors maintained that women who insisted on self-determination were dangerous to society because the obsession with developing the brain starved the uterus; even if she should wish to marry, such a woman would be sterile. During Browning's lifetime Dr

Thomas Clifford Allbutt (1836–1925) published papers in which he argued that nervous disorders in both men and women were on the increase, asserting that 'the stir in neurotic problems first began with womankind'.

Walter Besant (1836–1901), another writer and journalist, wrote that 'at no time has any woman enriched her world with a new idea, a new truth, a new discovery, a new invention [or] composed great music'. He went on to argue: 'The sun is masculine – he creates. The moon is feminine – she only reflects.' These ideas were of course not new and can be seen in Christian traditions. In the first book of the Bible, it is Eve who tempts Adam and it is she who takes the blame for the fall from grace. Only Adam is made in God's image; Eve is created from his rib. In *Paradise Lost* Book 8, John Milton writes that woman is for Adam 'Thy likeness, thy fit help, thy other self,/ Thy wish exactly to thy heart's desire' (450–451).

In conventional terms, as portrayed by Ruskin, women were created by God to be 'angels of the house' who should create for their husbands 'a place of Peace; the shelter, not only from all injury, but from all terror, doubt and division' (*Sesame and Lilies*). Women were taught that they must be passive, obedient and, even within marriage, asexual. Ironically, in the Victorian period prostitution was at a high level, and the double standards that judged men's behaviour by completely different rules from women's were widely accepted.

Ruskin, in *Sesame and Lilies*, projected the hope of national redemption onto the perceived purity of women who were excluded from the power drives of an industrialized and commercial society. Men, he argued, were 'wounded' and 'hardened' in the outside world, whereas women remained intact at home, and 'wherever a true wife comes, this home is always around her'.

Activity

How does Browning expose Victorian male anxieties about women in his poetry?

Discussion

In *My Last Duchess* and *Porphyria's Lover*, as we have seen, Browning portrays women through the voice of men. In these poems both women are silenced by a man asserting his power in the most extreme way. It is made clear to the reader that in *Porphyria's Lover* the woman is murdered to prevent her from choosing her *vainer ties* (24) instead of the speaker; in the speaker's own mind, he is helping to keep her pure. Porphyria is portrayed as a sensual woman in the poem, and is characterized by an unspoken passion and sexual desire. The poem concludes with the speaker attempting to vindicate himself with his reflection on how God will sanction his deed.

In *My Last Duchess* Browning again shows the reader an arrogant male speaker. The fact that he has immortalized his wife in art reveals a desire to contain and constrain her. He has captured her physical beauty, putting it behind a curtain that he controls, while eliminating her will and her capacity for action. Male anxiety about female sexuality is shown in the way the Duke describes his horror that his wife should smile at other men. She is portrayed as wanton and insensible of the glory of his name.

Interestingly, when Browning uses the voice of a woman in *The Laboratory*, she is callous, scheming and vengeful. However, unlike the male murderers in his poems, this woman has to pay a man to concoct the potion that will rid her of her rival; and again the murder victim is female. Like the women in the other two poems the speaker can be seen as sexually provocative, as she invites the unsavoury apothecary to *kiss me, old man, on my mouth* (46). In his characterization of this woman Browning exposes Victorian male anxiety about self-determined women; consumed by jealousy, the speaker is cruel and calculating, and takes a perverse delight in watching the preparation of the poison. This woman is not silenced, but she is presented as the antithesis of Ruskin's 'angel of the house'; she is a woman who is powerful and acts on her erotic desires.

Communication between men and women

In keeping with Victorian ideas concerning women and their place in society, Browning rarely gives women a voice to respond to the accusations, attitudes and behaviour of the men in his poems. In *My Last Duchess*, there is no communication between the Duke and his Duchess. The male voice is foregrounded and the woman is silenced; the Duke reveals that he has not discussed his feelings of disapproval with his wife as he arrogantly believes it would be beneath him. It is only when she is transformed into a work of art that the Duke can commune with his Duchess, as her living presence was too threatening.

Similarly, in *Porphyria's Lover* the male speaker's need for control and his apparent anxieties concerning Porphyria's sensual nature lead him to strangle her. Once again there is little sense of dialogue between the two, but the speaker's extreme insecurity is foregrounded. In these poems Browning explores male anxieties as he creates characters who are unable to communicate with women and allow them any self-determination. The women are powerless when confronted by the male who seeks to enslave his partner and refuses to enter into a dialogue.

Interestingly, in *The Laboratory*, Browning does create a female who is seen in dialogue with another man; however, this is not her lover but the apothecary who will dispense the poison to murder her rival. She covers her face with a mask, which remains firmly in place until the last eight lines of the poem. The mask is to protect her from the poisonous fumes, but symbolically it disguises her identity and gives her a licence to speak. She is no longer the aristocratic lady but the murderer seeking to destroy her rival in love. She cannot express her love, fears, or anxieties to the man she desires, and is silenced within her own class; her only audience is the humble apothecary.

Both of the pairs of poems *Love in a Life* and *Life in a Love*, *Meeting at Night* and *Parting at Morning*, are also, as we have seen, about lovers seeking each other. Their communication is indirect, at best – it is an avowal of their desire for each other, as in the last lines of *Meeting at Night*, where the lovers greet each other with *a voice less loud, thro' its joys and fears,/ Than the two hearts beating each to each!*

Activity

Explore the way Browning presents communication between men and women in *Andrea del Sarto* and *The Bishop Orders His Tomb at Saint Praxed's Church*.

Discussion

In *Andrea del Sarto*, Lucrezia is presented as the audience for Andrea's monologue, but she is not given the opportunity to reply to him, so the reader hears only the male speaker's perceptions. Andrea regards Lucrezia as his beloved muse, but also as his undoing. Like the other male speakers he seems to desire ownership of her, wishing to *frame your face in your hair's gold* (175). Andrea is gentle towards her and presents her as the central figure in his tragedy. She is silent in the poem, but ironically her silence seems to reflect her power, as she appears confident of her power over men and at the same time lacking in respect for her husband. She does not listen attentively, as he is forced to acknowledge from the outset: *You turn your face, but does it bring your heart?* (4). Even though the reader never hears Lucrezia's voice, it is apparent that she dominates him and his only concern is to satisfy her whims. The lack of communication in this poem, culminating in her departure at the final line, gives us a key to the tragedy of a man who is aware of the illusory nature of Lucrezia's love and his own moral inadequacy. He feels that he has been guilty of both weakness as a man and failure as an artist.

In contrast, the Bishop in *The Bishop Orders His Tomb* refers to his sons' mother as if she were nothing more than an acquisition he was proud of, along with his villas and his baths. He seems to accuse her of greed when he describes how her eyes used to *glitter... for my soul* (105), and one of his few comforts on his deathbed seems to be that he won her while his rival Gandolf envied him. The woman is, of course, long dead and therefore silenced at the outset, and she becomes simply another aspect of his grotesque pride as he dismisses her: *she is dead beside,/ Dead long ago, and I am Bishop since* (6–7), but his last words are of her: *so fair she was!*

The philosophy of the imperfect

The 'philosophy of the imperfect' was one that Browning shared with Ruskin and others among his contemporaries. This is the belief that life can only be lived fully if one attempts to achieve something that is almost certainly beyond one's powers, and so is destined to fail. The idea is most famously expressed in the lines from *Andrea del Sarto*, *a man's reach should exceed his grasp,/ Or what's a heaven for?* (97–98). Paradoxically, the failed attempt at impossible perfection in itself becomes an achievement as the individual is tested and extended beyond his limitations. What remains at the end is the value of the struggle.

This idea is explored in *Andrea del Sarto*, where the speaker presents himself as a failure both as a painter and as a man – the tragedy of the poem is that he realizes these failures as artist and lover are inextricably linked. The poem has the ironic subtitle *Called 'The Faultless Painter'*, and we see Andrea's self-assessment as a painter whose work is technically accurate but reveals no spiritual insights. Similarly, Andrea sees his wife Lucrezia's physical perfections and is saddened by her less than loving behaviour.

This painting of about 1528–1530 by Andrea del Sarto was once thought to be a self-portrait, but is of his friend Becuccio the glassmaker

The imagery of the poem is characterized by a gentle sadness and greyness: *A common greyness silvers everything* (35). Andrea insists that all is *Placid and perfect with my art* (99). However, ironically the perfections Andrea sees in his art and in his wife's beauty are in fact a measure of his limitations. When Andrea states that *a man's reach should exceed his grasp,/ Or what's a heaven for?*, Browning is suggesting that heaven is complete and perfect whereas the temporal world is characterized by imperfection and loss. If an artist understands this, he should have a greater insight into eternal values. In contrast an artist whose work is faultless and complete in itself can be guilty of seeing nothing beyond the temporal. Art that is superficially perfect fails, whereas art that is imperfect yet whose *soul is right* (113) succeeds because it challenges the viewer or reader to complete it and hence experience what the painter/poet has experienced.

Activity

Consider the presentation of the 'philosophy of the imperfect' in *Andrea del Sarto* and *Fra Lippo Lippi*.

Discussion

Although both poems take the form of dramatic monologues, they each have an informal structure that reflects the personalities and wandering thoughts of the speakers. Thus the form can reflect Andrea del Sarto's feelings of failure and also his moral confusion.

This is also seen in the shifting meaning of the imagery associated with gold. When Andrea is at the French court, gold is associated with energy, vitality, creativity and insight, as suggested by the phrase *fire of souls* (160). However, when Andrea leaves the court, gold becomes associated with the colour of Lucrezia's hair, in other words external appearances and the perfection of outward beauty. Finally gold becomes associated with money, and Andrea's compromises with a world that sets a monetary value on his art. Thus we are left as readers with an image of a man who is unfulfilled and unable to offer any sense of the perfection of heaven.

Fra Lippo Lippi is fully conscious of the discrepancy between his view of life and the views of those around him, but seems more at ease with this situation. He is aware that his particular outlook on life is open to misinterpretation. Lippi challenges formal attitudes to art, as his painting is characterized by depicting real people in all their physical presence. Lippi accepts that people are made in the image of God, and sees it as the painter's duty as well as pleasure to portray individuals as they are and allow the viewer to attempt to engage with the very essence of life itself.

It is through an intense engagement with the real and the imperfect that perfection can be glimpsed. As Lippi asserts, *Can't I take breath and try to add life's flash,/ And then add soul and heighten them threefold?* (213–214). Here *breath* seems to represent a person's physical presence, *life's flash* is what the painter does with his art to make his picture life-like, and *soul* is what the painter reveals about the essence of life in his painting.

The difference between *Andrea del Sarto* and *Fra Lippo Lippi* in terms of the philosophy of the imperfect is that Andrea's paintings are in themselves and in a limited way faultless, and in consequence offer no possibility of opening up a viewer's perceptions further. Lippi is able to make the viewer look again and more closely at the familiar, and to offer the viewer a sense of higher purposes.

Browning develops the philosophy of the imperfect on a more metaphorical level in 'Childe Roland to the Dark Tower Came'. The protagonist is concerned not simply with the end result of his mission to find the tower, but with the nature of his trials and whether he will be equal to the challenge, and also with the true meanings of success and failure. In this poem Browning explores the idea of self-doubt and the possibility of ultimate meaninglessness.

Activity

Look again at 'Childe Roland to the Dark Tower Came' and consider the ways in which Browning explores the idea of the conflict between the struggle to overcome one's limitations and the reality of self-doubt.

Discussion

The poem opens in an atmosphere of uncertainty as the speaker questions the truth of the directions he has been given by an old man. The speaker characterizes himself as a victim of deception, and the language of the poem reinforces this atmosphere of fear and doubt as the speaker talks in the opening line of being *lied* to, and then of attempts to *ensnare* him (8). The alliterative simile *skull-like laugh* (10) introduces the idea of death, and the reader has a disquieting image of a man lost in an unfathomable world where no one can be trusted and there is no real sense of direction or purpose.

Finding himself in this wasteland, the speaker nevertheless makes the choice to take the path of danger, *that ominous tract which, all agree,/ Hides the Dark Tower* (14–15), thus revealing that he is prepared to extend himself beyond his limitations and to embrace the imperfect in pursuit of an unknown perfection. Childe Roland acknowledges that he has no hope of success, but he asserts paradoxically *I hardly tried now to rebuke the spring/ My heart made, finding failure in its scope* (23–24). These lines create an image of the heart fluttering with excitement at the idea of an end, even though that end is likely to be failure. This sense of inevitable failure is reinforced by the speaker's allusion to those who have gone before him, *The knights who to the Dark Tower's search addressed/ Their steps – that just to fail as they, seemed best* (40–41).

Unlike many of the heroes of classical and medieval literature, the speaker reveals the very human quality of self-doubt. His doubt is not about whether he should continue in the task he has set himself, but rather about whether, in the face of either failure or success, he will be equal to the challenge: *And all the doubt was now – should I be fit?* (42). Childe Roland's honour is engaged as he is *Pledged to the plain* (50), but even his sense of commitment is in doubt as the descriptions of the landscape through which he passes, through the use of the pathetic fallacy, show him entertaining suicidal thoughts and experiencing unremitting despair. Throughout the poem any sign of optimism is almost immediately replaced by despair, and the journey he makes leads him further into a nightmare world, created by such images as the *dead man's cheek* (122), *Toads in a poisoned tank* (131) and *wild cats in a red-hot iron cage* (132).

Throughout the poem Browning uses the landscape to reflect the state of mind of Childe Roland, and the speaker also expresses feelings of despair, as he presses on and on yet feels *just as far as ever from the end!* (157). The mood of desperation is reinforced by a sudden address to the reader as the horrified speaker wonders how a range of mountains, *ugly heights*, could have *stolen in view* to encircle him, and challenges us to *solve it* (166–167). Once again we feel the conflict between the speaker's determination to embrace the challenge and his over-burdening fear that he can have no faith in his own judgement.

However, the poem concludes in a fusion of success and despair. Browning creates a tableau, as Childe Roland approaches the long-sought tower, of those who have gone before him and appear now as if in *a living frame* (200), but *each of old/ Lost, lost!* (197–198). However, the final lines of the poem create a kind of epiphany as the speaker blows his horn and Browning returns the reader to the simple statement that forms the title of the poem. Childe Roland is now *Dauntless* (203) at the culmination of his quest; even if he has been daunted many times along the way, he has not faltered and it is this attribute that is celebrated, not success or any meaning attached to the finding of the Dark Tower. What remains is simply the human determination to push beyond limits and embrace challenges.

In the poem *Apparent Failure*, Browning chooses to reverse the reader's expected response and to demonstrate that an attitude we take for granted – in this case, our ideas about the victims of suicide – may fail to take sufficient account of life's complexities. The title itself alerts the reader to Browning's view, and he builds a case not only for accepting the choice the suicides have made, but of seeing them as blessed.

Activity

In what ways does Browning explore in *Apparent Failure* the true meaning of success in human lives?

Discussion

In this poem, as elsewhere, Browning confronts the reader with the paradox that the consciousness of failure is in fact a measure of success. In *Apparent Failure* we are offered tableaux of the possible histories of the three men who now lie cold and lifeless on the *copper couch* (25). The speaker directly addresses the dead bodies he sees before him and imagines the contrast between the reality of their lives, perhaps living under *Some arch, where twelve such slept abreast* (35), and the hopes and dreams of their imaginations. Perhaps they had had grand ambitions; the speaker imagines that the first man had *wanted to be Buonaparte/ And have the Tuileries for toy* (38–39). He then engages with the imagined quest of the second dead man to fight for equality and justice as a *socialist* and *leveller* (42, 43), but clearly life has defeated this man also. The final portrait is of a man who has been trapped by the need for money to allow him to satisfy his desire for women.

In all three portraits we see individuals who have struggled to attain the unattainable. They are all men whom *God made* (28) and each one had a personal quest (see the next page for a discussion of the importance of this idea in Browning's poetry). Browning celebrates the value of each of them and suggests that their death is only an *apparent failure* because they were men who had a vision of what their lives should be and refused to accept a lesser reality; the fact that they rejected a life of failed dreams can be seen as evidence of strength of purpose. It is from this philosophical viewpoint that Browning expresses a *hope* (58) that value can be recovered even from such tragedies, *That, after Last, returns the First* (60), and *That what began best, can't end worst* (62).

As the poem concludes, the reader is left with a sense of Browning's refusal to measure people by conventional standards of achievement. He seems to suggest that people may have merits of a kind that the world does not recognize, and what is to be valued is not worldly success but the perpetual struggle and hopeful fight. Thus he concludes that *what God blessed once*, the creation of humanity, cannot *prove* to be *accurst* (63).

The quest

The concept of the quest is a traditional one in medieval courtly tales of men proving themselves through fulfilling daunting tasks and persevering through adversity as fearless warriors, usually to win the love of a beautiful woman. The protagonists are usually driven by the idea of conquest, either of an enemy or of monsters that are symbolically depriving them of freedom or of a woman's love; often they journey in search of a precious object, place or person. Browning appropriates this tradition and explores it in different guises in his poetry.

In 'Childe Roland to the Dark Tower Came', as we have seen, Browning deals specifically with one aspect of the quest: the perilous journey through a wasteland to find something that is hidden. However, Childe Roland's quest seems less concerned with his apparent object than with seeking some kind of spiritual fulfilment or regeneration. Throughout the poem he expresses concern over his fitness for the task in hand, and his fitness even to fail in a heroic way. Clearly this links with Browning's philosophy of the imperfect (see page 175) as well as engaging the reader with the psychology of the speaker. This quest, then, is primarily a journey into the self. The wasteland can be seen as symbolizing the horrors within Childe Roland's mind, and when he reflects on the sins of Cuthbert and Giles, whom he is now representing, he identifies with them. In this poem Browning presents the quest as a journey towards self-knowledge and self-awareness, as Childe Roland faces up to the demons within, perhaps summed up in the overriding symbol of the Dark Tower.

In other poems Browning uses imagery of the quest to explore the idea of choices made on life's path, and the way these affect the whole of an individual's life. In *The Last Ride Together*, the woman has chosen not to continue with the relationship; however, the speaker takes a curious satisfaction in the ride itself, and in it recognizes what is almost an *instant made eternity* (108), that is, a moment of fulfilment that can become eternal in the sense that it convinces him his life's quest has not been in vain.

The idea of the quest for a moment of happiness that can be made to last takes a grotesque turn in *Porphyria's Lover*, as this can only be achieved by strangling Porphyria. In a similarly self-deluding quest, the Duke in *My Last Duchess* seeks to achieve final control over his wife by reducing her to a work of art.

We have already seen Browning's presentation of love in *Love in a Life* and *Life in a Love* as a never-ending quest by two people to truly find each other and find fulfilment in their relationship (see page 162).

Religion

Throughout his life Browning remained convinced of the sacredness of the visual imagination, and saw it as a medium through which one could connect with God. In contrast Ruskin argued that whereas medieval life 'was inwoven with white and purple: ours is one seamless stuff of brown' (*Modern Painters*). He ascribed this dulling of life's colours to 'our want of faith'. The Victorian period was one in which many people began to feel doubts about traditional religious beliefs in the face of scientific advances and social changes. Browning, apart from a short period in his teenage years, seems to have retained an unshaken faith in God. His belief that God was the author of everything was crucial to the way he saw himself as a poet.

Like Wordsworth, Browning believed that it was through nature that God could be seen in the world. Nature, he believed, was a divine creation, and it was a poet's engagement with the natural world that gave him the vision to see 'Not what man sees, but what God sees' (*An Essay on Percy Bysshe Shelley*, 1852). Thus Browning saw his writing as a form of engagement with God, and like painting he believed it evoked a response from the reader that involved a keen sense of God's purposes working through creation. As Fra Lippo Lippi asserts:

> This world's no blot for us,
> Nor blank; it means intensely, and means good:
> To find its meaning is my meat and drink.

(313–315)

Here, of course, Lippi is referring to his paintings, but the words can also be applied to Browning's view of his poetry and his connection with God. However, Browning cannot be described simply as a Christian believer, as in his poetry he adopts various stances, none of which gives a clear view of his religious beliefs. In the dramatic monologues, people who have taken their beliefs to extremes are often portrayed in an unfavourable light. He often allows his speakers to express views with which neither the poet nor the reader may sympathize, and he refrains from expressing his own beliefs.

Poetry was the medium through which Browning felt he was able to offer a sense of the divine, in contrast to the conventional thinking of the mid-Victorian age in which rational intellectual pursuit was seen as the way to engage with the mysteries of God. Browning celebrated the physical nature of human beings and believed that human intuition operated through the emotions, not the intellect. In *Fra Lippo Lippi*, the speaker asserts *If you get simple beauty and nought else,/ You get about the best thing God invents* (217–218). To Browning, flesh and the spirit were natural allies and the two were inextricably bound together. Faith, to him, was not a matter of blind belief but rather springs out of what Wordsworth called 'a passionate intuition', instincts we are born with. Wordsworth asserts in *Ode on Intimations of Immortality* that we come into the world 'trailing clouds of glory', and it is this sense of the divine that Browning believed could be cultivated throughout life, as something separate from rational intellectualism.

Activity

Consider the ways Browning presents his ideas about the soul being linked to the flesh in *Fra Lippo Lippi*.

Discussion

In *Fra Lippo Lippi* Browning creates a monk, a man theoretically devoted to the spiritual, who passionately engages with the body and the senses. In many ways Lippi represents the spiritual bound up with the material and physical world; these are seen as stepping stones to a realization of the spirit. Lippi exclaims:

> – The beauty and the wonder and the power,
> The shapes of things, their colours, lights and shades,
> Changes, surprises, – and God made it all!
>
> (283–285)

Through the character of Lippi, Browning celebrates the glory of God to be found in the world around us. Lippi shows his scorn for the limited views of the clergy who dismiss his work because it shows *Faces, arms, legs and bodies like the true* (177). Lippi's response to those who insist that he *Rub all out, try at it a second time* (194) illustrates Browning's belief that the divine is to be found in the physical world: *A laugh, a cry, the business of the world... And my whole soul revolves, the cup runs over* (247–250).

In *Prospice*, Browning addresses the traditional religious subject of the challenges to be faced when confronted by death. Characteristically, however, he focuses on the importance of the idea of the quest and the need to be fully involved even in the experience of dying. In contrast to the tone that concludes many poems, for example 'Childe Roland to the Dark Tower Came', in *Prospice* Browning ends on a note of certainty; he expresses confidence that, having wrestled with death, his reward will be to be reunited with his beloved wife, and there will be a consciousness of *peace* after *pain*.

Activity

In what ways does death in *Prospice* take the form of a struggle in which the speaker is sure of a final victory?

Discussion

The defiant tone that opens this poem engages the reader with Browning's insistence on maintaining the quest and allowing the power of the imagination to embrace even the most terrifying experience, the moment of death. There is no sense of a passive surrender to the inevitable, but an active engagement with what he terms a *battle* (11). Browning asserts that he is content to *pay glad life's arrears* (19) and wishes to experience every aspect of dying, insisting that *I would hate that death bandaged my eyes, and forbore,/ And bade me creep past* (15–16). Death may be terrible, but the speaker insists that he wishes to *taste the whole of it* (17).

Browning depicts the struggle with death through imagery connected with extreme weather: *snows, blasts* (3), and *the press of the storm* (5). There is also personification of death as *the foe* (6) and the *Arch Fear in a visible form* (7). The syntax of the poem, which is fragmented in places, reflects the inner turmoil of the speaker as Browning develops the idea of a personal battle. However, the rhythm of the alternating long and short lines, and the regular rhyme scheme, suggest that although the speaker struggles he has a definite purpose, and that there is to be a *reward of it all* (12).

Later in the poem the reader is presented with a nightmare world in a similar style to that of Childe Roland, with images of wild storms and devils with *fiend-voices that rave* (23). However, as the poem reaches a climax of horror the mood changes and the tone becomes almost lyrical. This alteration in mood is created partly through the use of anaphora (repetition), as the horror of the storm and the devils *Shall dwindle, shall blend,/ Shall change, shall become first a peace out of pain* (24–25). The language suggests a kind of rebirth, signalled by the image of a *light* (26), a Christian symbol of hope for life after death. Browning concludes with a moving image of his belief that *The reward of it all* (12) is nothing less than the union of two souls, his own with that of his departed wife, and a real sense of pathos is created as he addresses his late wife and asserts *I shall clasp thee again* (27), and that *the rest* lies *with God* (28).

Appearance versus reality

In many of his poems Browning explores the problem of separating what is illusory from what is real. In *Andrea del Sarto* the speaker attempts to maintain the illusion of a happy marriage, but is constantly troubled by the reality of Lucrezia's lack of concern for or even interest in him. The tragedy for Andrea lies in the conflict between his hopes and his fears, his successes and his failures. On the one hand he presents his relationship as positive and clearly plays the role of a traditional lover, describing Lucrezia's hand as *a woman of itself,/ And mine the man's bared breast she curls inside* (21–22). However, at some level he knows that she is estranged from him and his only way of maintaining their relationship is to provide her with money: *I'll pay my fancy* (226). If he behaves foolishly for her sake, he admits it is *as I choose* (266). She deserts him for the *Cousin's whistle* (267) and he is left to comfort himself with his attempt at maintaining the illusion not only of love, but of success in his art.

In *The Bishop Orders His Tomb at Saint Praxed's Church*, the Bishop must maintain the illusion that he is a man of religion. He displays Catholic learning and loves the aesthetic aspects of the religious life, admiring the mosaics of angels in the *aery dome* (23) and the beauty of the rituals. However, Browning shows us a man who does not acknowledge the truth about himself and his

The church of Santa Prassede in Rome inspired Browning to write *The Bishop Orders His Tomb at Saint Praxed's Church*

values. He uses a style of speech that suggests he is a man of learning while also implying a lack of moral depth. He is both materialistic and sensuous, and he moves quickly between the spiritual and the material: *Ever your eyes were as a lizard's quick,/ They glitter like your mother's for my soul* (104–105). The Bishop appears to have created for himself a public character that is opposed to his real personality. Even approaching his death he is concerned with appearances and speaks as if weakness and death belong to his mistress and his rival Gandolf, while he has strength and life.

As the poem moves towards its conclusion, Browning shows the Bishop is frustrated by his powerlessness to influence his sons, much less to make them truly care for him, and it causes him to question whether his life has been anything more than a dream. The Bishop sees life as a matter of fighting *With tooth and nail* (16) for what you want, whereas death is passivity. We are left with the paradoxical image of the Bishop endlessly striving for advantage and for activity, while he is about to become fixed symbolically in marble.

Activity

Consider how Browning explores the theme of appearance versus reality in some poems of your choice.

Discussion

In *The Last Ride Together*, Browning explores the speaker's determination to maintain the illusion of love as he tries desperately to eternalize the fleeting moments of togetherness with the woman he loves. The speaker idealizes the relationship and attempts to convince himself that it is possible to freeze the moment, as in a work of art, to maintain the illusion that his lady loves him.

In *My Last Duchess* and *Porphyria's Lover* both speakers maintain the illusion that their behaviour is acceptable and that they can escape human judgement and even the judgement of God. Both men are presented as being obsessed with achieving the appearance of fidelity in their lovers and maintaining the illusion of complete power over women, rather than accepting the realities of a mutual relationship. In their different ways they each preserve the physical appearance of their murdered lovers. This is in contrast to Browning's ideas about ideal love being the consummation of an intuitive process by which lovers transcend the barriers of their individuality and achieve spiritual union. The illusory nature of the relationships in *My Last Duchess* and *Porphyria's Lover* is revealed through the speakers' obsession with themselves and their desire to possess and fix, rather than engage with, a partner.

Form, structure and language

Dramatic monologues

Browning is, of course, renowned for his use of the dramatic monologue, in which he attempts to reveal a complex personality through a speaker's own words. Oscar Wilde, in *The Critic as Artist*, wrote that Browning was fascinated not with thought itself but with the processes of thought, and this is clearly seen in the dramatic monologues. By adopting this form Browning was able to capture an individual's thought processes at one moment in his or her life; the speakers unwittingly reveal themselves and their true motivations to the reader, who 'overhears' them speaking to an imagined audience. The speakers are always unaware of how much they are giving away about themselves. In consequence there are no definitive conclusions or resolutions, but Browning creates the impression of each personality continuing along the same path beyond the end of the poem.

Browning achieves these effects by creating a tone of conversational intimacy, through the language chosen and the use of dramatic pauses and enjambment (run-on lines). A good illustration of this is the opening lines of *My Last Duchess*, in which we 'overhear' the Duke saying *That's my last Duchess painted on the wall,/ Looking as if she were alive*. The position of *Looking* at the beginning of a line highlights on the one hand the idea of the illusion of life in the Duchess, while on the other creating a sense of the woman's presence in the room as she appears to be *Looking* at those who stare back at her. The poem uses a fairly regular iambic rhythm (an unstressed followed by a stressed syllable), which echoes the rhythm of everyday speech. Whenever this rhythmic pattern is broken, the reader is alerted to a particular mood or tension in the poem. Thus when a word such as *Looking*, with its stress on the first syllable, begins a line it changes the rhythm, gives the words energy and extra emphasis.

Browning experiments with a variety of forms, which he uses to reflect the minds of various speakers. Browning bases *Fra Lippo Lippi* on blank verse, which is unrhymed iambic pentameter (five pairs of unstressed and stressed syllables); but snatches of songs are inserted, as seems appropriate for the encounter described in the poem. Childe Roland, on the other hand, recounts his story in rhyming six-line stanzas with irregularly stressed pentameter lines. The language in this poem at times appears harsh and unpoetic, but it serves to reflect the hellish journey of the knight. In contrast *Andrea del Sarto* is a poem in blank verse that offers the reader the musings of a defeated man. The language is controlled, the mood calm, and the regular iambic pattern mimics natural speech. *Porphyria's Lover* has a patterned rhyme scheme, perhaps suggesting the madness concealed within the speaker's reasoned self-presentation.

Poems such as these are 'spoken' by an individual, but what the reader hears is not one voice but two: the voice of the speaker and that of the poet. These voices constantly merge with each other and the reader is caught between feelings of sympathy for and moral judgement of the speaker. This is seen clearly in 'Childe Roland to the Dark Tower Came'; Browning uses the landscape and the language of the Gothic horror tradition to create a mysterious world but also to explore the complexity of human experience. The poem draws on images of ugliness and disease in nature: *Bog, clay and rubble, sand and stark black dearth* (150), the *palsied oak* (154) and the mountains, *Mere ugly heights* (166). The language used to describe the landscape reflects the tortured mind of Childe Roland as he metaphorically journeys into the darkness of his own mind while physically struggling through the desolate wilderness.

Browning often counterpoints colloquial, familiar language with heightened terms, to communicate his characters' personalities as well as the natural movement of their thoughts and feelings. For example, the speaker in *Up at a Villa – Down in the City* adopts a conversational tone throughout the poem. Through the use of exclamations such as *by Bacchus* (4), colloquial phrases such as *Well now* (7), and the use of simple rhetorical questions such as *Why?* (11), Browning creates a sense of a character who is personally engaged with a conversation about everyday life. Similarly the opening of *Fra Lippo Lippi* immediately engages the reader with the character. Lippi's colloquial expressions, as in *clap, Zooks, harry out,* and *gullet's-gripe,* serve to create the image of a lively man who is interested in people and has a zest for life. But Lippi is also eloquent on the subject of *The beauty and the wonder and the power* (283) of the world, and of his art. His description of his first work of art on the monastery walls reveals his appreciation of the vividness of daily life, as he describes children gazing at a murderer, the bereaved son crossing himself while still violently angry, and the girl who is in love with the *brute* and offers all that she can in his aid. Through these rich and vivid descriptions, Browning reveals his character's vitality and love of life, and it is these qualities that the artist pours into his paintings, just as Browning does in his poetry through his rich and varied language.

Activity

Choose one dramatic monologue and explore the ways in which Browning uses language and style to depict a particular personality type.

Discussion

In *The Laboratory* Browning explores the jealous and vengeful reaction of a woman who is disappointed in love. As with the other monologues the silent listener is important, and in this case it is the apothecary, who is selling his services by supplying poison to this woman. Browning, as is often the case, chooses to set the poem in the past, and highlights this by the use of the subtitle *Ancien Régime,* which refers to the government of eighteenth-century France. The effect of this setting is to distance the poem from Victorian attitudes and values, and therefore allow Browning to explore the extremes of jealousy and obsession. He also uses this distancing effect in *My Last Duchess* and *Porphyria's Lover.* The setting of the latter is perhaps more contemporary, but it is nevertheless set apart from society.

The Laboratory is written in 12 stanzas of four lines each and has an ordered rhyme scheme of *aabb.* The dominant rhythm is anapaestic (two unstressed syllables, followed by a stressed syllable), and a rather jaunty effect is created, which one might think is not in keeping with the subject. The poem therefore appears melodramatic, even approaching the comic, as the character's behaviour and attitude appear not just malign but outrageous. The rhythm can also be regarded as reflecting the woman's highly excited state of mind; it creates an energetic and intense movement in the verse, and a sense of urgency. The speaker's calculating approach to the deed she is about to commit, and her desire to see her victim suffer (*Not that I bid you spare her the pain*, 37) suggest a mental state that is extremely disturbed.

Interestingly, Browning's frequent use of alliteration − such as *Pound at thy powder* (10) and *Brand, burn up, bite* (39) − both lightens the tone and suggests the woman's petty spitefulness, as if she is spitting out her words. He also uses onomatopoeia in phrases such as *Grind away, moisten and mash up* (9) to suggest the energy of the apothecary and the speaker's relish as she watches him prepare the poison. The rhyme scheme also helps to develop the reader's awareness of the perverted delight the speaker feels as she watches the preparation of the potion; this is seen particularly in the rhyming of *paste* with *haste* (9–10) and *treasures* with *pleasures* (17–18).

As the monologue develops, the reader is given insights into the way the speaker sees her rival, and the poem develops an image of this woman as both scornful and manipulative. But the reader is left to question the reliability of the narrative voice, since we know that she is driven to bitter rage at being rejected by her lover. The speaker presents herself as being at a disadvantage, describing herself as a *minion* (29), which suggests not just being small in stature but also subservient and weak. Browning explores how such a woman might gain revenge in a world where her gender makes her powerless and it seems that only through stealth can she settle her scores.

Throughout the poem Browning contrasts the luxury and opulence of the court with the grim setting of the laboratory, and it is within this setting that the speaker seems to come alive. She is no longer the *minion* but gives a powerful and, one might argue, erotic impression. In the final stanza she invites the unsavoury apothecary to *kiss me, old man, on my mouth if you will!*, while simultaneously offering him *all my jewels* so that he may *gorge gold*. This woman is clearly in tune with both the sexual and monetary desires of the man she has chosen to deal with, and we are left with an image of a determined, albeit unbalanced character.

However, the final line of the poem returns the reader to the aristocratic world: *next moment I dance at the King's*. This reminds us of the social context in which the speaker lives, and we are left to question her lightness of tone in contrast to the darkness of the deed she intends to commit.

The shorter poems

Browning often wrote paired poems, and there are two examples of pairs in this collection. *Meeting at Night* takes the form of a lyric (a short poem that offers a condensed idea or emotion). This poem is characteristic of Browning's style in that he liked to use colloquial words, and at times adopt a straightforward tone. In *Meeting at Night* the sand is described as *slushy* (6) and the lighted match is seen to *spurt* into flame (10). Through this simple language, Browning conveys complex emotions, and in this particular poem sexual intensity is suggested through the use of images and the circling rhyme scheme *abccba*. In contrast, *Parting at Morning* consists of only four lines with a regular metrical pattern, and the rhyme scheme *abba*, and the very brevity of the poem suggests the sudden extinguishing of the flame of love. The image of the sun offers the idea of a masculine world of work and material gain, rather than the delights of passionate encounters.

Love in a Life is another short poem in which Browning condenses his thoughts into two stanzas. There is a complex rhyme scheme and the lines are of varied length, which serves to reflect the confusion of the speaker in his quest for love. The idea of the quest (see page 181) is placed in a domestic setting, but the repetition at the beginning, *Room after room*, reinforced by the rhyme at line 6, sets the mood of the poem as the speaker seems to be trapped in an endless, fruitless pursuit for a love that will never be realized. This idea is developed in *Life in a Love* as Browning adopts an assertive, almost obsessive tone through his use of the simple short question and answer that open the poem. Again the rhymes are complex; the first three lines rhyme with the final three, while the other lines follow *abba* and *abab* patterns. The whole poem is characterized by a jerky rhythm that reflects the passion and emotional intensity of the speaker.

This use of varied metrical, rhyming and stanzaic patterns is particularly characteristic of Browning's style, and he insisted that his poetry was 'always dramatic in principle, and so many utterances of so many imaginary persons, not mine' (Preface to *Dramatic Lyrics*, 1842). Thus even in his shorter poems the reader often hears a dramatic voice offering a perspective on some aspect of life.

The more formal structure of *Love Among the Ruins* offers a series of contrasts between the rural and the urban world. This poem has a rhyme scheme where pairs of long and short lines rhyme together, and on the whole they are full masculine rhymes (one-syllable words), which gives the poem a staccato rhythm. They way that each short line follows and is balanced against a longer one often gives the impression of a supplementary thought being added, in a conversational style. Browning creates short tableaux of a time now past, and recreates the energy, passion and fervour of the *million fighters* with their *thousand chariots in full force* (74–76), in contrast to the rural idyll of the present. His use of apostrophe at the conclusion of the poem, *Oh heart! oh, blood that freezes, blood that burns!*, emphasizes the futility of such aggression in contrast to the triumph of love, and Browning characteristically concludes his poem in simple style with the uncompromising assertion: *Love is best.*

In *Prospice*, as we have seen (page 185), Browning also uses pairs of long and short lines, but here there is an alternating rhyme scheme. Once again full masculine rhymes are used, and here they seem to convey a sense of closure and containment which, together with the staccato rhythm, reinforces the sense of the speaker's isolation in the face of death.

Activity

Explore the ways Browning uses language and form in *Home-Thoughts, from Abroad*.

Discussion

In some ways this poem, although 20 lines long, is like a sonnet as it divides into two sections of which each has a slightly different tone, and ends on a striking note that sums up its message. This innovative style was characteristic of Browning, who liked to experiment with different forms and styles. The two stanzas have different rhythms and rhyme schemes. In the first stanza the tone is wistful as the speaker longs for home. This is created through the metrical pattern in which the first two lines are in trimeter (a meter consisting of three iambs per line), followed by two tetrameter lines (a line of four metrical feet), three pentameter lines (a five-iamb meter) and then a concluding trimeter line. The rhyme scheme is *ababccdd*; this creates a kind of rising and falling tone in the poem, reflecting the emotional tempera- ture of the speaker, who moves from joy and delight when he thinks of home to a sad resignation because of his distance from it.

The second stanza is longer and is written almost entirely in pentameter, apart from line 16, which is in trimeter. It begins with a rhyming couplet, moves to an alternating rhyme and then back to couplets. The more even metrical pattern creates a contemplative tone. In this stanza the poet considers the natural cycle of the season, which occurs despite his absence.

The language Browning chooses echoes the celebration of nature seen in earlier writers of the Romantic era, as well as embracing the pastoral tradition by creating a rural idyll. Throughout the poem Browning uses images of birds, the *chaffinch*, the *white-throat*, the *swallows* and the *wise thrush*, to bring to life the busy activity of the countryside in spring. This is complemented by the description of the *blossomed pear tree* (11) which is seen as fertile and beautiful as it *Leans* in a familiar and carefree way over the field.

The delicate beauty of England is celebrated throughout the poem as it appears in the speaker's imagination and memories, until the last line, which offers a contrast in tone and mood. There is a pause in the speaker's thoughts, signalled by a dash, and all at once the reader is presented with a vivid comparison between England and Italy through the image of *this gaudy melon-flower*, which we imagine the speaker pointing to in his immediate surroundings.

Characterization and setting

Setting

Browning's poetry experiments not just with the presentation of character but with the variety of settings that he chooses to create. In 'Childe Roland to the Dark Tower Came', for example, Browning constructs a romantic atmosphere as he experiments with ideas from the Gothic tradition. The tone of the poem is strengthened by the description of natural scenery, but interestingly there is little suggestion of the supernatural. However, Browning achieves an overall atmosphere of horror by placing natural objects in a particular setting. The weeds, the lack of animal and vegetable life, the old horse and even the river itself become, in the context of the setting, things of horror. The transformation of the landscape into a setting suggestive of horror is achieved partly by putting it into the context of the knightly quest, but a sense of menace is created through the vision of the hills, which appear first as animals *locked* in struggle (177) and then as *giants at a hunting* (190). The concluding sound of the horn acts as an audible revelation of horror and of Roland's self-knowledge, as it calls out into the dark and desolate landscape. Browning symbolically fuses mindscape with landscape here.

Similarly in *Porphyria's Lover*, Browning uses the darkness of night and the tempestuous weather to create an atmosphere of unease and also of Porphyria's ghostly and unpredictable energy.

In contrast, in *Fra Lippo Lippi* Browning uses a setting in the streets of fifteenth-century Florence. In this poem the reader is invited into the world of Renaissance art, characterized by patrons such Cosimo de Medici and the rich palaces and churches that dominate the world of the working artist. Through the use of this setting Browning exposes the corruption and superficiality of the rich and of the ecclesiastical world, while giving life to the painter's personality through his use of images

Cosimo de Medici, the wealthy Florentine patron of the arts, painted by Jacopo Pontormo

characterized by colour, as if working with an artist's palette. In *Andrea del Sarto*, Browning uses the speaker's memories of a setting at the French court, with its ostentatious display of gold, to suggest vitality, creativity and insight, and this is contrasted with the reality of his present world, one characterized by *A common greyness* (35). Andrea's limitations are exemplified through the contrast created between his golden days at the French court and his present moral confusion.

In the death-bed scene in *The Bishop Orders His Tomb at Saint Praxed's Church*, Browning explores what Ruskin refers to as 'the Renaissance spirit, – its worldliness, inconsistency, pride, hypocrisy, ignorance of itself, love of art, of luxury, and of good Latin' (*Modern Painters*). The darkness of the room and the fading candlelight are used to suggest the approaching death of the speaker, and the fact that the Bishop lies in limbo between the world of the living and that of the dead offers a setting in which other characters appear and disappear with the sharpness of a nightmare.

The idea of the nightmare world is used differently in the setting of *My Last Duchess*, where the reader is plunged into the constrained formality of the court of the Duke of Ferrara. Just as in *The Laboratory*, Browning sets his poem in the past, thus distancing it from Victorian attitudes and values and freeing himself to explore the extremes of obsession and murderous behaviour. Through the setting Browning evokes the Duke's world, peopled by his dead wife, his future wife and the emissary of his future father-in-law. The picture of his dead wife is conjured up before the reader like an apparition or a ghostly figure in a dream, and the descriptions of her daily life provide a vivid sense of the settings in which these people lived.

The use of an unusual and striking setting in which to explore ideas about life is seen in *Apparent Failure*. The morgue on the banks of the Seine is not presented as macabre, but as a resting place for those who have chosen to take their own lives; the speaker asserts that he is struck by the *reverence* (29) of the place. Just as the subject matter of the poem is a paradox, so too is the setting, as the speaker begins by describing how he *plucked up heart and entered* (15), but once inside he perceives that in fact this is the men's *proper place of rest* (33).

In *Love Among the Ruins* Browning uses a rural setting with ancient ruins to explore the contrast between the political aggression of the urban world and the natural passions of love and sexual desire. The rural setting of *Two in the Campagna* allows Browning to explore the possibilities of an alternative space away from the limitations of the urban world. It is in this natural scene that the speaker attempts to capture both the wandering thoughts that escape *Just when I seemed about to learn!* (56) and the fleeting moments of communion with his lover. The pastoral setting, however, is not the ideal and wholly natural place the speaker had hoped it would be; part of its beauty lies in *yonder weed* and *Some old tomb's ruin* (14). Similarly, thought processes and relationships are too complex and imperfect to be contained. The use of the pathetic fallacy in the setting of *Meeting at Night*, which features a seascape, allows Browning to engage the reader by implying the burning passion of the lover's quest.

In *Home-Thoughts, from Abroad* and *'De Gustibus –'*, Browning brings to life the glory of the English countryside through rich and colourful portraits of gentle, idealized country scenes, contrasting them with the more rugged and romantic Italian landscape and the anarchic energy of Italy.

Characterization

One of Browning's great skills is to engage the reader in such a way that in his poems we feel we are listening to a living person and catching not only a tone of voice, but subtle movements of the mind. The characters he creates, particularly in his dramatic monologues, build up a kind of intimacy with the reader as Browning conveys their shifting moods in thought and speech. Browning provides us with a gallery of characters, many from historical times and distant places, but all nevertheless revealing human strengths and weaknesses.

In *My Last Duchess* and *Porphyria's Lover*, the reader listens to the words of outrageously self-obsessed characters, but paradoxically it is their wickedness and lack of self-knowledge that makes them fascinating to the reader. In these two characters Browning explores the extremes of human nature and touches on the fine line between sanity and madness. The Duke of Ferrara has a connoisseur's pride in the beauty of his Duchess, but ironically it is this same pride that causes him to murder her. In *Porphyria's Lover* the speaker offers intimate revelations about his relationship with Porphyria and betrays his conceit in his belief that he is above judgement. Browning maintains a tension between the sympathy we feel for his characters and the moral condemnation that they may deserve.

In *The Bishop Orders His Tomb at Saint Praxed's Church* Browning offers us a complex character who is troubled by inner conflicts that he doesn't himself understand. The Bishop's world may be limited, and his options are now confined to the choice of stone for a tomb, but we are nevertheless given a complete study in human pride and superficiality. The paradox of the poem lies in the tension between the way the Bishop views himself and the way the reader is invited to engage with his character, and to sympathize with his evident failures in human relationships. Emotionally and intellectually limited, he is nevertheless depicted as a cultured man, which only serves to make more striking his use of the traditional vocabulary of the Church to speak of the material rather than the spiritual world. He is clearly unable to understand the full significance of the opening line he speaks – *Vanity, saith the preacher, vanity!* – and as his character develops, Browning offers us a picture of a man who is keenly aware of material values but not of the value of his closest relationships.

In all but two of the monologues in this collection there is a male speaker; however, in *A Woman's Last Word* and *The Laboratory* Browning explores a female character in an equally dramatic situation. The speaker in *The Laboratory* is no less disturbed and malign than some of Browning's male characters – she is presented as cruel and calculating in her desire for revenge. However, Browning alerts us to her feminine qualities in the way she responds to the colour of the poison she is to purchase, and her desire *To carry pure death in an earring, a casket,/ A signet, a fan-mount, a filigree basket!* (19–20). The mention of such female adornments completes the portrait of a courtly, aristocratic young woman, and makes her perversion even more shocking, certainly to Browning's contemporary audience. Unlike the seemingly calm detachment of the Duke of Ferrara and Porphyria's lover, this character is presented as being in a highly excited state of mind. She is not only attempting to orchestrate a murder but is exploiting her sexuality to gain the murder weapon she needs. The fact that the poem closes with her invitation to the apothecary to *kiss me, old man, on my mouth if you will!* suggests she is not just manipulative but also sexually voracious.

Many of Browning's other poems create snapshots of individuals that enable him to explore particular themes and ideas. In *The Patriot*, for example, Browning uses the character of a heroic leader to depict the fickle nature of public opinion, whereas in *The Lost Leader* he depicts a man who has compromised his principles and abandoned those who believed in him. In *Love Among the Ruins* he uses a pastoral setting and a shepherd to explore ideas on love and the contrast between the urban and rural life, in the tradition of pastoral writing. In *The Last Ride Together* Browning uses the speaker to engage the reader with ideas about the failure of love and his doctrine of the philosophy of the imperfect. Thus through his portrayal of various characters, Browning is able to explore diverse aspects of human life and, particularly in the monologues, his poems offer a particular perspective on life through different individuals' experience of it.

Activity

Choose one poem and explore the importance of the setting and Browning's presentation of the main character.

Discussion

Childe Roland is a character who from the outset is highly dramatized. Through him we are introduced to other characters who, as in Browning's other poems, remain silent yet direct the experience and thoughts of the main character. The poem begins in an elusive way as the opening words are *My first thought was, he lied in every word*. We are not told that Childe Roland has asked for directions nor that he is on a quest for the Dark Tower. In this way Browning creates a mystery that is slowly unravelled throughout the poem.

The setting is important to the development of the character as the mind of Childe Roland is revealed through his reactions to the landscape and the situation he finds himself in. He seems to be on a journey of self-discovery as he struggles through the wilderness, constantly battling with his own conscious and unconscious apprehensions, and the reader is engaged with him in his apparently endless ordeal. The horror and the menace that surround him act as a catalyst to action, and his determination is reinforced through Browning's images of a world of desolation and horror.

The character is ultimately defined in terms of the chivalric quest, as he is defiant in the face of failure, and the concluding lines of the poem insist that he remains undaunted. His final action in blowing his horn is not explained, and seems forlornly purposeless, yet strangely life-affirming and moving. As the poem closes the reader feels that Childe Roland has not been defeated and the fact that he has continued to wrestle with the horrors he is confronted with means that by the time he reaches the Dark Tower he has achieved some kind of successful closure.

Critical views

Browning became well known for *The Pied Piper of Hamelin*, published in *Dramatic Lyrics* in 1842, but in the early years his

This cartoon of Robert Browning as the Pied Piper was drawn by Frederick Waddy in 1873

work did not meet with critical acclaim (see pages 2–6). Much of it was considered to be obscure or difficult. Despite this adverse reaction he published several collections of verse between 1841 and 1846. It was with the collection *Men and Women* (1855) that Browning seriously attempted to court success. As we have seen on page 9, he asserts in a letter of 1853 that the collection he is writing is to be 'a first step towards popularity for me'.

Unfortunately, many critics still dismissed his work as obscure or in bad taste. However, the collection was well received by both the artists of the Pre-Raphaelite movement (founded in 1848 by William Holman Hunt, John Everett Millais and Dante Gabriel Rossetti) and the intelligent younger readers at the universities, and it was the voice of the young that went on to influence the taste of the coming decades.

His 1864 collection *Dramatis Personae* and his epic *The Ring and the Book* (1868–1869) finally gained him full public recognition. A 'Browning Society' for the appreciation of his poetry was formed in 1881, eight years before his death. His reputation by then was assured, and he was buried in Poets' Corner in Westminster Abbey.

Robert Browning's memorial in Poets' Corner, Westminster Abbey

Browning is regarded today as one of the most 'modern' and influential of mid-Victorian poets, and is valued for the energy in his poetry and his willingness to experiment with different forms and subject matter.

There is never going to be just one reading of a poem, as each of us comes to literature with different values, attitudes and expectations. A Victorian reading of Browning's writing would naturally be quite different in some respects from that of a modern reader, as the reader would bring different experiences and beliefs. All literature and works of art are open to different interpretations, and in this section we will consider two particular ways of engaging with a text. One will look at a Marxist approach and the other a feminist one.

Marxist theory

A Marxist approach challenges the idea that we bring free and independent minds to the reading of a book. In the Preface to *Towards a Critique of Political Economy* (1859), Karl Marx argues that 'The mode of production of material life conditions the general process of social, political, and intellectual life'. Here he is suggesting that the way a society generates money (in Victorian England, as today, by means of a capitalist system) determines the way individuals think and write. He goes on: 'It is not the consciousness of men that determines their existence, but their social existence that determines their consciousness'. Marx therefore stresses the importance of the economic base of society, that is to say the way an economy is organized, which determines its 'superstructure'. The superstructure can be broadly defined as education, law, religion, philosophy, political ideas and the arts.

This theory is completely at odds with the thinking of writers such as Matthew Arnold (1822–1888), who believed individuals were free thinkers and came to the interpretation of literature with no preconceptions. Marxist thinkers assert that thought is subservient to and follows the material conditions under which it develops. Marx insisted that capitalism only thrives because it exploits its workers, and in consequence human beings become alienated, since they are only defined in terms of their contribution to production.

Marx was writing during the same period as Browning. He saw that men who had been skilled workers, such as blacksmiths, cobblers and farmers, were forced to take up factory work where they became just one link in a long chain and lost any sense of identity with the fruits of their labour. To sustain a capitalist economy, material need has to be created, and in consequence, Marx argued, individuals are encouraged to worship the false god of money and materialism, becoming increasingly alienated.

Activity

Consider how you might apply a Marxist reading to some of Browning's poems.

Discussion

In *The Bishop Orders His Tomb at Saint Praxed's Church*, we are shown a man whose life has been dominated by his love of material possessions. Browning offers a study of a man who, even on his deathbed, is unable to move beyond the limitations of his acquisitive nature as he worries about the size and importance of his tomb. Clearly in this poem it is possible to offer a Marxist reading as we see a man who, although he is a Bishop, has no real engagement with his spiritual self. His concern is with his villas, baths and works of art, and even his relationship with his sons and their mother seems to be tainted by the pursuit of material things, and his pride in the woman's physical beauty. Here then, it is possible to argue, is a man who is alienated and whose life has been damaged by distorted materialist values.

Similarly in *Andrea del Sarto*, the speaker lives in mental torment because of his desire to provide a lavish lifestyle for his wife. The *common greyness* that *silvers everything* (35) in Andrea's life, it can be argued, stems from a sense of alienation. He is no longer in control of his life or his art, as all are driven by the need for material gain and the desire to provide for his demanding wife. This is illustrated near the beginning of the poem, where he is shown not to be his own master: *I'll work then for your friend's friend, never fear,/ Treat his own subject after his own way* (5–6).

The lack of control over his work and the necessity of being at the command of others is also a theme of *Fra Lippo Lippi*, as the speaker

explains he is in the pay of Cosimo de Medici, and has little control
over the subjects he paints. This is emphasized when he asserts:

> I've been three weeks shut within my mew,
> A-painting for the great man, saints and saints
> And saints again.

(47–49)

Lippi is therefore another example of a man who cannot achieve self-
determination even in choosing the subject of his art, but is at the
mercy of those with power and money. The speaker in *Pictor Ignotus*
is also a victim of those who *buy and sell* art (50). He has withdrawn
from their world, at great personal cost.

Feminism

In a similar way to Marxist theory, the feminist movement insists
that socio-historical influences determine the production of all
literature. Feminist thinkers argue that in literature written by
men, male characters are exploitative and repressive in their rela-
tions with women. They argue that women are negatively stereo-
typed in films, advertising and rock videos to this day.

An important writer in this field is Kate Millett who, in her
book *Sexual Politics* (1970), suggests that in the male writers she
has studied there is an important link between sex and power. In
terms of power, sexual acts that we would consider to be private
are in fact an extension of the public realm. Therefore the private
and the public sphere cannot be separated, and feminist critiques
reveal how representations of women often repeat cultural
stereotypes and are male constructions. In many works of literature, the dominant ideology represents female independence as a
negative thing, while helplessness and the renouncing of ambition are presented as admirable qualities in women. The message
offered to women, according to these theorists, can be summed
up as: dependence leads to being indulged, while independence
results in rejection.

Activity

Apply a feminist reading to some Browning poems of your choice.

Discussion

In *My Last Duchess*, Browning does not offer the reader the female perspective; throughout the poem the Duchess's voice is silenced. The Duke possibly implies that she is sexually voracious, as symbolized by what he describes as her *earnest glance* (8). The fact that she *thanked men* and *all and each/ Would draw from her alike the approving speech* (29–31) is presented by the Duke as justification for her murder. In keeping with the prevailing attitudes and values of his society, the Duke feels justified in his actions as his wife is not content to be simply an extension of himself, but takes pleasure in other aspects of life.

The whole poem embodies the idea of the male gaze, as both the Duke and the silent envoy can be imagined to stare at the portrait in which she has been captured. The Duke is in control of the portrait, and is empowered by the fact that the woman is no longer a threat.

Similarly, Porphyria is given no voice in *Porphyria's Lover*, and she also is presented as sensuous and passionate, mainly through images of fire and warmth. The description of her removing her *dripping cloak* (11) and loosening her *damp hair* (13) suggests a provocative woman. This is compounded by her actions, as the speaker describes how *She put my arm about her waist* (16). Here, it can be argued, is a picture of a dangerous woman, one who is prepared to take the initiative and to make demands upon her lover. A feminist reading might suggest that the male speaker feels threatened, even emasculated by her behaviour, and the only way he can redress the balance is to destroy her. Once dead she becomes the doll-like creature he has desired, passive and under his control. He evidently feels re-empowered as he asserts:

I propped her head up as before,
Only, this time my shoulder bore
Her head

(49–51)

In *The Laboratory*, Browning offers a female voice but interestingly it is a cruel and vindictive one, and in many ways he uses the stereotype of the fury of a scorned woman. This woman once again reveals a sense of independence and a determination to empower herself. However, Browning does not offer a sympathetic representation of the woman's misery; rather she is demonized and her motives appear ignoble.

A feminist reading might suggest that Browning deliberately disempowers the female speaker through her association with luxury and her provocative behaviour, thereby demanding a negative reaction.

Women and Roses can be read as a study of male fantasies, with the speaker referring to the women dancing in a kind of choreographed order: *They circle their rose on my rose tree*. By repeating this line throughout the poem, with its possessive pronoun *my*, he signifies his control. At times the women are presented as demanding, as the speaker asks how he can *Break my heart at your feet to please you* (19). The poem is characterized by sensual language and a longing for *eternities of pleasure* (34). Each tableau of a group of women corresponds to images of male desire; the women vary from the alluring but unattainable to virgins not yet born, who offer all the promise but none of the threat contained in living women. A feminist reading might stress the lines in which the poet expresses the desire for ultimate control over a woman: *I will make an Eve, be the artist that began her,/ Shaped her to his mind!* (46–47).

Alternative readings

Using theories is one way of addressing different interpretations, but it is probably more fruitful to look at layers of meaning within the text itself. To explore layers of meaning it is necessary to look closely at the language used and to consider how it may be read in different ways.

An example might be a reading of the lines *As I gain the cove with pushing prow,/ And quench its speed i' the slushy sand* from *Meeting at Night* (5–6). On the one hand the surface meaning is describing the motion of the boat in the water, but the lines can also be seen as creating a sense of urgency and sexual passion by using terms that are suggestive of a sexual act, in images such as the *pushing prow* and *slushy sand*.

Equally, themes or ideas in a poem may offer alternative readings. Readers may have varying levels of sympathy with the characters in poems such as *My Last Duchess* and *Porphyria's Lover*; these poems may be read as studies in obsessive love or jealousy, or male anxiety and inadequacy. There are many ways to interpret a poem, and as readers we need to engage with layers of meaning and not limit ourselves to one interpretation.

Activity

Consider some words, phrases, imagery or themes and ideas that can be seen to have alternative readings in a poem of your choice.

Discussion

Love in a Life opens with the lines *Room after room,/ I hunt the house through*. On the one hand, it can be argued that from the outset of the poem Browning alerts the reader to the idea of an exciting quest. However, it is possible to detect a sense of boredom as the speaker seems to be listlessly searching the rooms to no avail.

Equally, the question near the end of the poem, *who cares?*, can be read as the speaker adopting a dismissive tone, becoming despondent, or perhaps feeling carefree as if his time and efforts are freely given.

A reader can also suggest alternative readings of the character of the speaker in *Andrea del Sarto*. On the one hand, it can be argued that Browning presents him as an unfortunate man with whom the reader deeply sympathizes; alternatively, he can be seen as one who has made mistakes in his work and his relationships, yet has achieved a large measure of success; the reader may consider the disappointments he feels to be unreasonable or purely of his own creation.

Essay Questions

Worked question

The question below is followed by some points you might address in your response.

To what extent do you agree with the view that through the speaker in *Andrea del Sarto* Browning presents a man who is the victim of a destructive woman?

This essay requires you to offer a balanced argument, so it is necessary to consider the various ways in which it is possible to read *Andrea del Sarto*. The following plan will offer you a guide to answering the question, but you will have your own ideas that you can add.

- The introduction should set up your argument.

- On the one hand Andrea is presented as a victim of Lucrezia's self-interested demands. On the other hand it is possible to read him as a man who is by nature characterized by self-doubt and a lack of belief in himself and his talents.

- The main section of the essay should explore these two readings. Remember throughout your essay to refer back to the question at regular intervals.

- Consider the voiceless presence of Lucrezia and examine how Browning presents her through the words of Andrea. You may wish to introduce a feminist reading and discuss how Browning offers us only the male view.

- Look at what Andrea says about his relationship with his wife, and his suggestion that had she given him *soul*, his paintings might have been characterized more by imagination than by his skill as a *faultless painter*.

- Explore the way Browning presents Lucrezia as a demanding woman, both in the opening of the poem and at its conclusion.

Consider the idea that the *Cousin* is in fact one of her lovers and that Andrea prefers to delude himself about her relationships rather than confront her, and in consequence possibly lose her.

• Consider how Andrea has acted, in terms of the way he has spent the money given to him by the French king to facilitate Lucrezia's desires.

• Turning to the alternative argument, look closely at the way Browning presents Andrea's character. Consider how he compares himself to other painters and looks for reasons as to why his work is not so inspired as theirs.

• Consider his need for a muse and the complexity of the presentation of Lucrezia; on the one hand she is presented as his inspiration, but on the other she is regarded as not fulfilling the painter's needs because, as he sees it, she lacks true commitment to him.

• Throughout, comment on details of the language and style Browning uses. For example, you might want to consider how he uses colour, and the way he refers to different shades to develop the character of Andrea.

• In your conclusion, it is not necessary to favour one side of the argument; clearly there are many layers of reading to be explored. You may wish to suggest that through the characterization of Andrea, Browning does not simply present the reader with a man who is the victim of a destructive woman, but gives us a study in human fallibility and the complexity of human relationships.

Sample questions

The following questions are for you to try.

1 Explore the ways in which Browning presents the difficulties of love through the speaker in *Andrea del Sarto*.

2   Explore the ways in which, in *The Bishop Orders His Tomb at Saint Praxed's Church*, Browning presents the reader with a man who cannot let go of the temporal world.

3   To what extent do you agree with the view that in *The Bishop Orders His Tomb at Saint Praxed's Church* Browning challenges Victorian attitudes to the clergy through his presentation of a Bishop who has little or no spiritual perception?

4   Discuss the ways Browning presents ideas about love in *Two in the Campagna*. Explore the effects of language, imagery and verse form, and consider how this poem relates to other Browning poems you have studied.

5   Discuss the ways Browning presents ideas about women in *Women and Roses*. Explore the effects of language, imagery and verse form, and consider how this poem relates to other Browning poems you have studied.

6   Explore the ways in which Browning uses landscape in '*Childe Roland to the Dark Tower Came*' both to create a sense of mystery and to explore the complexity of the human psyche.

7   What do you consider to be the significance of Browning's use of pictorial art in *Fra Lippo Lippi*?

8   To what extent do you agree with the view that it is Browning's descriptions of the scenes that surround Fra Lippo Lippi that give his character vitality and humanity?

9   Discuss the ways Browning presents ideas about the quest in *Apparent Failure*. Explore the effects of language, imagery and verse form, and consider how this poem relates to other Browning poems you have studied.

10   Discuss the ways Browning presents ideas about art in *Pictor Ignotus*. Explore the effects of language, imagery and verse form, and consider how this poem relates to other Browning poems you have studied.

11   How far do you agree with the view that the Duke in *My Last Duchess* is a study of male insecurity?

Essay Questions

12 Consider Browning's use of the portrait in *My Last Duchess*, and explore the way it is used to reveal the Duke's inability to connect with life.

13 Explore the ways in which Browning creates a ghostly and sinister atmosphere in *Porphyria's Lover*.

14 Discuss the ways Browning presents ideas about Italy in *Up at a Villa – Down in the City*. Explore the effects of language, imagery and verse form, and consider how this poem relates to other Browning poems you have studied.

15 Discuss the ways Browning presents religious ideas in *Prospice*. Explore the effects of language, imagery and verse form, and consider how this poem relates to other Browning poems you have studied.

16 How far do you agree with the view that in *The Patriot* Browning presents the reader with a study on the fickle nature of humankind?

17 In what ways do you feel Browning creates a character with whom the reader is able to empathize in *The Patriot*?

18 In what ways do you feel *Love Among the Ruins* can be read as a declaration of love for Elizabeth Barrett Browning?

19 Consider the importance of the use of landscape in *Love Among the Ruins*.

20 Discuss the ways Browning presents ideas about communication between men and women in *A Woman's Last Word*. Explore the effects of language, imagery and verse form, and consider how this poem relates to other Browning poems you have studied.

21 Discuss the ways Browning presents ideas about patriotism and leadership in *The Lost Leader*. Explore the effects of language, imagery and verse form, and consider how this poem relates to other Browning poems you have studied.

22 Consider how Browning explores ideas about life and art in *The Last Ride Together*.

23 To what extent do you agree with the view that the lover in *The Last Ride Together* is more concerned with himself than with the woman who accompanies him?

24 Explore the ways in which Browning creates sexual tension in *Meeting at Night* and *Parting at Morning*.

25 Compare and contrast the ways in which Browning presents the idea of the quest in *'Childe Roland to the Dark Tower Came'*, *Love in a Life* and *Life in a Love*.

26 Consider the ways in which Browning adopts the style of the earlier Romantic poets in *Home-Thoughts, from Abroad* and *'De Gustibus –'*.

27 What do you consider to be the strengths of Browning's use of the dramatic monologue? In your answer, refer to at least two poems.

28 Referring to at least two poems of your choice, explore the ways in which Browning develops ideas on appearance versus reality.

29 Browning spent a large portion of his life in Italy. In what ways do you see this reflected in his poetry?

30 Browning was known to have loved painting and sculpture; how do you feel he uses this passion in his poetry?

Chronology

1812	Robert Browning born 7 May at Camberwell, London, son of Robert and Sarah Anna (*née* Wiedemann) Browning.
1814	Browning's sister Sarianna born.
1828–9	Browning attends London University.
1833	Publishes *Pauline*.
1835	Publishes *Paracelsus*.
1837	Publishes *Strafford*; the play is performed at Covent Garden with William Macready.
1838	Visits Italy for the first time.
1840	Publishes *Sordello*.
1841	Publishes *Bells and Pomegranates* Volume 1.
1842	Publishes *Bells and Pomegranates* Volumes 2 and 3 (*Dramatic Lyrics*).
1845	Meets Elizabeth Barrett. Publishes *Bells and Pomegranates* Volume 7 (*Dramatic Romances and Lyrics*).
1846	Marries Elizabeth Barrett and moves to Italy.
1849	Birth of son Robert Wiedemann Browning (nicknamed Pen or Penini). Death of Browning's mother.
1852	Publishes essay on Shelley as an introduction to *Letters of Percy Bysshe Shelley*.
1855	Publishes *Men and Women*.
1861	Death of Elizabeth Barrett Browning. Returns to live mainly in London.
1864	Publishes *Dramatis Personae*.
1866	Death of Browning's father. From this date Browning lives with his sister Sarianna.
1867	Awarded honorary MA by the University of Oxford; becomes honorary fellow of Balliol College.
1868–9	Publishes *The Ring and the Book*.
1873	Publishes *Red Cotton Night-Cap Country*.
1879–80	Publishes *Dramatic Idyls*.
1881	Foundation of the first Browning Society.
1889	Publishes *Asolando*. Dies in Venice, 12 December, and is buried at Poet's Corner, Westminster Abbey.

Further Reading

Biography

The Letters of Robert Browning and Elizabeth Barrett. 1845 to 1846
(2 volumes) (Harper and Brothers, 1899)

Critical books and articles

Isobel Armstrong (ed.), *The Major Victorian Poets:
Reconsiderations* (Routledge and Kegan Paul, 1969)
Isobel Armstrong (ed.), *Robert Browning* (Bell and Sons, 1974)
Philip Drew (ed.), *Robert Browning: A Collection of Critical Essays*
(Methuen, 1966)
Northrop Frye, *Anatomy of Criticism: Four Essays* (Princeton
University Press, 1957)
Robert F. Garratt, 'Browning's Dramatic Monologue: The
Strategy of the Double Mask', *Victorian Poetry* Vol. 11 No. 2
(Summer 1973), pp. 115–25
Park Honan, *Browning's Characters: A Study in Poetic Technique*
(Yale University Press, 1961)
Ian Jack, *Browning's Major Poetry* (Clarendon, 1973)
Henry James, 'Browning in Westminster Abbey', *The Speaker* 4
January 1891, pp. 11–12
Robert Langbaum, *The Poetry of Experience: The Dramatic
Monologue in Modern Literary Tradition* (Norton, 1963)
William O. Raymond, *The Infinite Moment and Other Essays in
Robert Browning* (University of Toronto Press, 1950)
Alan Sinfield, *Dramatic Monologues* (Methuen, 1977)
Clarence Tracy (ed.), *Browning's Mind and Art* (Oliver and Boyd,
1968)
W.C. DeVane, *A Browning Handbook* (Appleton-Century-Crofts,
1955)

J.R. Watson, *Browning: 'Men and Women' and Other Poems: A Casebook* (Macmillan, 1974)

Journals

Journals dedicated solely to Browning include:
Browning Society Notes
Browning Institute Studies
Studies in Browning and his Circle

Websites

http://www.browninglibrary.org/
http://www.browningsociety.org/
http://www.victorianweb.org/